THE
NEGOTIATION
PLAYBOOK

THE
NEGOTIATION
PLAYBOOK

Strategies That Work
and Results That Last

Glin Bayley

WILEY

First published 2025 by John Wiley & Sons Australia, Ltd
© John Wiley & Sons Australia, Ltd 2025

The right of Glin Bayley to be identified as the author of *The Negotiation Playbook* has been asserted in accordance with law.

ISBN: 978-1-394-28468-9

A catalogue record for this book is available from the National Library of Australia

Registered Office
John Wiley & Sons Australia, Ltd. Level 4, 600 Bourke Street, Melbourne, VIC 3000, Australia

For details of our global editorial offices, customer services, and more information about Wiley products visit us at www.wiley.com.

Wiley also publishes its books in a variety of electronic formats and by print-on-demand. Some content that appears in standard print versions of this book may not be available in other formats.

Trademarks: Wiley and the Wiley logo are trademarks or registered trademarks of John Wiley & Sons, Inc. and/or its affiliates in the United States and other countries and may not be used without written permission. All other trademarks are the property of their respective owners. John Wiley & Sons, Inc. is not associated with any product or vendor mentioned in this book.

Limit of Liability/Disclaimer of Warranty
While the publisher and author have used their best efforts in preparing this work, they make no representations or warranties with respect to the accuracy or completeness of the contents of this work and specifically disclaim all warranties, including without limitation any implied warranties of merchantability or fitness for a particular purpose. No warranty may be created or extended by sales representatives, written sales materials or promotional statements for this work. This work is sold with the understanding that the publisher is not engaged in rendering professional services. The advice and strategies contained herein may not be suitable for your situation. You should consult with a specialist where appropriate. The fact that an organisation, website, or product is referred to in this work as a citation and/or potential source of further information does not mean that the publisher and author endorse the information or services the organisation, website, or product may provide or recommendations it may make. Further, readers should be aware that websites listed in this work may have changed or disappeared between when this work was written and when it is read. Neither the publisher nor author shall be liable for any loss of profit or any other commercial damages, including but not limited to special, incidental, consequential, or other damages.

Cover design by Wiley
Cover Image: © Aleksandr Bryliaev/Adobe Stock

Set in Plantin Std 10.5/16pt by Straive, Chennai, India
Printed and bound by CPI Group (UK) Ltd, Croydon, CR0 4YY

C9781394284689_021024

This book is dedicated to you, the reader, and our collective journey of becoming, in pursuit of a more compassionate and collaborative world.

Contents

About the author

Hi, I'm Glin Bayley. Those who know me well—or those who read my weekly personal blog, Glin & Tonic—already know that I'm more likely to share candid stories of my lessons in life and the mistakes I've made than to boast about my achievements. However, as you'll learn from reading this book, the perception of our value matters not only in our own eyes, but in the eyes of our audience. Authority and social proof are key principles in influencing this perception.

I've spent over 18 years mastering the art and science of negotiation, both consciously and unconsciously, since my first formal training in the subject. Today, I help individuals and teams unlock their potential in this crucial skill. As a negotiation consultant and trainer, I've had the privilege of working with large global enterprises, guiding individuals and teams to achieve transformative results through value-driven strategies.

My professional journey began in commercial finance, working with global food and beverage brands, negotiating with stakeholders, including suppliers and retailers, in sales, buying and procurement.

After a move from England to Australia and nearly two decades in finance, my deep interest and curiosity in self-leadership and human behaviour led me to leave my executive finance career and start my first business, Heart of Human. I work predominantly with senior corporate women as an executive coach, helping them develop their self-leadership and inner confidence to be unstoppable. Through my interactions with clients, I have learned how much a lack of confidence and self-doubt can hold so many incredible women back from negotiating their worth.

This experience led me to an incredible opportunity with a global negotiation consultancy, training teams to negotiate more effectively. During that time, as a recovering 'Type A' achiever with a huge drive for performance, I had the profound realisation that negotiation skills are a significantly under-utilised personal and professional superpower. They not only improve performance, communication and relationships, but also give us the confidence to have any conversation.

This led me to start my second business, The Value Negotiator, helping individuals and organisations navigate the complexities of negotiation with confidence and creativity. I focus on developing the skills of commercial business-to-business negotiation as well as on who people become through the process. I truly believe that negotiation isn't just about what you do, but *who you* become in the process.

In addition to my consulting and training work, I serve as a non-executive board director for a non-profit organisation, furthering my commitment to making a positive impact in the community.

Writing *The Negotiation Playbook* has been a labour of love and necessity. It's driven by my desire to share insights and strategies that have already transformed my clients' lives and businesses. While my stories may not involve the high-stakes drama of hostage negotiations, I believe they are more relatable to the everyday lives we all lead. I believe that everyone has the potential to be a great negotiator in a way that doesn't compromise their ethics and values, and this book is my way of providing you with the tools and mindset to succeed.

When I'm not immersed in the world of negotiation, you can find me walking barefoot on the beaches of the Sunshine Coast of Australia with my toy cavoodle, Noah; with my head buried in a personal growth book, deepening my spiritual practises; having deep and meaningful conversations with friends; or writing my weekly blog, Glin & Tonic, where I share reflections and lessons learned from my personal life journey.

Thank you for taking the time to read this book. I'm grateful for the opportunity to show you that *when you understand how to make agreements well, the most powerful agreements are the ones you make with yourself.*

Acknowledgements

First and foremost, I need to acknowledge you, the reader. Thank you from the deepest depth of my heart. You're the reason I wrote this book. It was you I kept in mind, along with visions of the opportunities you would create for yourself and your business, that kept me going when I felt overwhelmed by the writing journey. Hearing your stories connected me to the need to write this book in the hope that, together, we'd lift the level of consciousness in the way people communicate and make agreements. I hope you find this a valuable read and use it as a resource on your journey.

Writing a book is rarely a solo journey. There are many incredible people who have supported this book coming to life.

First is my partner, John. Before the inception of the idea, John encouraged me to take the plunge and book myself into a writers' retreat to explore whether I had a book idea worth pursuing. He's been a willing and gracious beta reader of every single chapter, ensuring the concepts made sense to someone from a non-corporate background. He kept me fed and watered, took care of everything at home, and supported me through a rollercoaster of emotions, keeping me sane. I will be eternally grateful.

Mum and my sister Rosie have been role models of courage and bravery, and a constant source of encouragement and support every time I take on a new big, hairy, audacious goal. Thank you for understanding my drive, keeping me grounded with the truth that I never have anything to prove, and reminding me to always choose happiness.

To Peter Baines and the Wildnest Writers Retreat: your thoughtful, explorative questions, expertise and guidance helped me develop my initial book proposal. The quality time and beautiful, nourishing space you and Claire created allowed me to sit with my ideas and get my thoughts on the page. Thank you for holding me accountable for getting my proposal and first chapter written and submitted. Your support has been invaluable—starting is always the hardest, and you showed me it was possible.

To Lucy Raymond, my executive editor, thank you for asking the difficult questions that helped shape this book. Thank you for believing in my vision and investing in me with the wonderful team at Wiley to bring it to life.

A huge thanks to my structural and copyediting team, Leigh McLennon, Chris Shorten and Melanie Dankel, for being so invested in helping me refine my ideas, for your meticulous attention to detail and for guiding me through the publishing process. You've helped me see the book in a new way and made it even more accessible to the reader.

A heartfelt thanks to Dr. Rosina McAlpine for your generous and valuable insights and guidance on the book writing process and for your support in reviewing my chapters and helping me with the instructional design of the book content. Your warmth and encouraging words made a daunting task much more achievable.

Lastly, I want to acknowledge the incredible people I've had the privilege of working with. Your stories and experiences have deeply inspired and greatly influenced the content of this book. Thank you from the bottom of my heart.

For the sake of brevity, not everyone, including dear friends, can be mentioned, but please know I see you and appreciate you.

My heart is overflowing with appreciation.

Warmest,
Glin

Introduction

When I was growing up, my mum spoke so little English that I became her unofficial translator, especially during those high-stakes moments when we were buying household goods and services! 'Ask them for a discount', she'd tell me in Punjabi, followed by a nudge and her timeless mantra, roughly translating to: 'What's the harm in asking?' While some might see this as just haggling, to me, it was a masterclass in understanding value, assertiveness and, oftentimes, the art of persistence.

As a single parent raising two daughters, my mum had no qualms in asking for what she needed. A resilient Indian mother driven by circumstance, she modelled courage and strength, leaning into any discomfort she felt to increase the possibilities of getting better value for her family. Those moments for teenage me, however, were excruciating. Indian or not, every teenager just wants to blend in, right?

But there I was, tasked with blending 'bargaining' into 'British retail etiquette'. I felt so uncomfortable asking, I thought I'd die from the embarrassment. Can you relate to my discomfort? If you took a moment right now to reflect on your comfort level with negotiating, would you say you love it, or would you avoid it even if your life depended on it? Over time, as I advanced in my teenage years, instead of getting more comfortable with being uncomfortable and following the brave example set by my mum, I sought to avoid the discomfort and stopped asking altogether. I shrugged it off as no big deal, but little did I know then that being able to negotiate is a very big deal indeed.

My teenage self didn't realise that she'd stepped away from developing a superpower, one that would have changed her world, and the world of those around her, for the better.

Do you want to develop a superpower? One that helps you understand yourself and others more clearly? A superpower that not only helps you and those around you achieve better financial outcomes, but helps you build stronger relationships both personally and professionally. One that will improve your career and business results, enable you to defuse objections and conflict situations, increase your self-confidence, and hear and see what others miss so that you can make a meaningful difference in the world. Would you choose to step forward or step away?

The power of negotiation, as you'll learn in this book, isn't only about what you can achieve, but more importantly, about who you become through the journey.

Imagine feeling confident in having any conversation, including difficult ones. Imagine asking for what you need and having the skills to get it. Imagine discovering insights that others miss because your perspective is clearer and your ability to connect the dots is more refined. Imagine staying calm in stressful environments and being able to de-escalate and defuse tension, regardless of the situation. You don't have to imagine this if you embrace the power of negotiation.

What to expect from this book

Given that this book is titled *The Negotiation Playbook*, you may naturally assume that it will guide you on how to negotiate more effectively—and it will. However, this book is not just about developing negotiation skills as something you *do*; it's intended as a pathway for who you can *become*.

What I've learned through the journey of developing negotiation skills is that the opportunity for personal growth is like no other. Imagine confronting a situation that triggers your deepest fears and being able to lean into that fear with confidence. The intellectual challenge of negotiation goes beyond just securing a good deal. It compels us to be intentional with every conversation in which we're seeking agreement. It challenges us to recognise our value and frame it in the context of others' needs and interests to maximise it. Negotiation challenges us to stop seeking external validation but instead honour what we have to offer by considering its usefulness and benefit to those around us.

This book is anchored around the theme of value, the exchange of which is the core premise of negotiation. It is my hope that this book helps you to become the 'value negotiator', both for yourself and your business. It's written to inspire you to be impactful in the way you conduct yourself, not just through your involvement in a process. It emphasises the importance of valuing relationships over transactions, and how to handle the dilemma that arises when both relationships and results matter. The essence of this book is to help you use negotiation skills to transform your day-to-day challenges in business and life into opportunities for shared rewards, to help you to explore deeper to solve smarter, and uncover the understanding that drives every deal.

Whether you're a corporate professional negotiating high-stakes deals; an entrepreneur or small business owner growing your business; a parent balancing family responsibilities with personal interests; a consumer in everyday situations, such as buying a home or a car; or an individual navigating personal relationships and major life decisions, there is something of value in this book for you.

Conversations to reach agreements, as we know, can be highly complex, involve high stakes and high emotion, and the outcomes of these conversations are often uncertain. It takes a brave soul to embark on the journey to master negotiation, because doing so requires you to learn how to master yourself. Imagine the impact you could have. You could transform the world around you just one conversation at a time. Imagine the agreements you could make if you were able to powerfully articulate your value in the context of the needs of others. That's the true power of negotiation.

Part I: Foundations of value-driven negotiations

The first half of the book lays the groundwork for understanding value-driven negotiations by addressing the fundamental questions that shape your approach:

- *Why we negotiate?* Explore the underlying motivations behind negotiation and its significance in both personal and professional contexts.

- *Which negotiator type are you?* Identify your negotiation style and understand how it affects your strategies and outcomes.

- *What to negotiate?* Identify negotiable elements and prioritise them based on your goals, while addressing and overcoming common beliefs that hinder effective negotiation.

- *Who matters in negotiation?* Learn to recognise key players and stakeholders and their roles in negotiation processes.

- *When to negotiate?* Choose the optimal times to negotiate to maximise your leverage and success.

- *Where to negotiate?* Understand the importance of setting in negotiations and how different environments can influence results.

Part Two: The 'how' of negotiating with the Value Method

The second half of the book introduces the Value Method, a strategic approach designed to keep VALUE at the forefront of your negotiations. Each element acts as a key, unlocking the full potential of your negotiation capabilities.

- *V: Identify the value.* Learn how to pinpoint the value you bring to the table and what you aim to gain from the negotiation.

- *A: Analyse the data.* Discover how to use data to inform your strategy, predict outcomes and prepare for various scenarios.

- *L: Understand your leverage.* Assess the power dynamics at play and learn effective ways to use your leverage.

- *U: Embrace being uncomfortable.* Find out how to maintain your composure and confidence in challenging or unfamiliar situations.

- *E: Execute the plan.* Implement your strategy with clear objectives and adaptability to changing circumstances.

In the final chapter, I share the essential values that successful negotiators embody and discuss what sets apart those who thrive as the Value Negotiator.

- *Values for successful negotiation:* Uncover the key values that drive effective negotiators and learn how to integrate these into your approach to stand out in any negotiation scenario.

How to use this book

You can read this book from start to finish or explore the sections that are most relevant to you at this time. Throughout the book I share personal and professional examples and provide ample opportunities for you to reflect on your own experiences and use the checklists to help consolidate your knowledge. Negotiation has many layers and mastering it isn't achieved overnight—it requires a commitment to practise. With this in mind, this book is designed to simplify the complex and make the challenging aspects of negotiation more accessible for those new to the field, while still offering valuable insights for seasoned negotiators who are open to discovering new perspectives or deepening their existing knowledge. Whether you are taking your first steps in negotiation or seeking to refine your skills, this book is your guide to becoming a more effective and insightful negotiator.

Part I

Foundations of value-driven negotiations

How you do one thing is an indication of how you do everything, which is why we're beginning with the foundations. Laying the foundations doesn't mean we're starting with the basics; if I've learned anything about negotiation intelligence, it is that it is anything but basic. My aim is to build your baseline of knowledge quickly so that when it comes to implementation, you have a solid base from which to develop your negotiation practise. I call it practise because, as with most skills, they only stay sharp with continuous development, and ongoing practise is necessary if you wish to reach a level of mastery.

To get the best from this book, my suggestion is to have a particular negotiation scenario in mind—either one you've previously experienced or one that you'd like to have. This way, you can relate the content in this book to your own context.

The 6 Ws

In Part One, we'll cover the core fundamentals: why, which, what, who, when and where. This simple framework helps you consider your own negotiation context, identify the need and take a more holistic approach to the core elements you need to consider. By the end of Part One you will be able to answer the following questions:

Why

- do you want to negotiate?

- do they want to negotiate?

- is this important to you and them?

Which

- negotiator type are you dealing with?

- communication style is most effective?

- issues are likely to be the most contentious?

What

- is the scope of the negotiation (i.e. what are the different levers)?

- behavioural strategy is appropriate: competitive or collaborative?

- mindset and beliefs do you need?

Who

- are you directly negotiating with?

- is the decision-maker?

- else is involved?

When

- do you expect to have the negotiation?

- would be the optimal timing?

- will you need to be fully prepared?

Where

- will the negotiation take place?

- would it be most conducive to reaching an agreement?

- is the least suitable place?

Chapter 1

Why we negotiate

Why negotiate? Because we can't maximise the value we get for ourselves and the value we give to others if we avoid it.

Negotiation is about maximising and exchanging value. When we're negotiating, we're aiming to maximise value—what's important to us—which includes the benefit we receive, our usefulness to others and the overall worth of what's being negotiated. The way in which we exchange value is shaped by our personal values as well as what is important to the other person or party.

We negotiate to exchange value

When it comes to the obvious benefits of negotiation, of course we want better financial outcomes for ourselves and our businesses. We want the confidence to ask for what we want and to get it. We want status, recognition and satisfaction at getting a good deal. We want to protect ourselves from being exploited by others, and we want to feel confident and powerful in the process.

It's important to understand that *value* is subjective; for example, if you're considering a new job, do you value flexible working hours over a higher salary? Or do you value a higher salary above everything else because you want to pay off a home or travel the world?

What we value reflects what's important to us. Our values are deeply personal and vary from person to person. Our values guide our behaviour, influence our decisions, and shape our interactions with others. We'll talk more about this in Chapter 12 when we look at values in negotiation.

However, through countless observations of people I have coached, and my own experiences in business and life, I've seen how easy it is for us to take, or destroy, value (more on this in Chapter 7) by adopting an oppositional approach in negotiation. Alternatively, in seeking to avoid being exploited or avoid our own discomfort, we end up trying to protect value, holding tight to what we already have. We all have those friends who stay in unfulfilling jobs because they believe they'll lose what they have if they ask for better. This approach to protecting value only serves to limit any opportunities to discover more. What's much harder to achieve is maximising the total value that could be available by creating and growing value, so there's more value to share. The problem is many of us just don't know how to achieve this win-win.

One of the key drivers of this, as I mentioned on page 10, is that the concept of value is often misunderstood. How can we communicate our value if we fail to understand what value is? After training hundreds of leaders, I've seen how cost, price and value are commonly thought of as being the same thing, but they're not. Price and cost are monetary measures that focus on a more transactional or economic perspective. While cost and price can change based on various demand-and-supply inputs in the market, the value of something can remain unaffected based on its importance, usefulness, benefit and worth to us. The value of having a safe roof over your head doesn't change because the rent, interest rates or purchase price of your home goes up or down.

Value can also increase and decrease, but its movement is determined by the importance, usefulness, benefit and worth to an individual or group, and is contextual to their needs and interests. A bottle of still water in the supermarket where there is an abundance of other options to choose from won't mean very much. But imagine we were lost in the desert with no food and water, and someone offered us a single bottle of water? We'd value it significantly more in this second scenario. While the costs may not differ much between the two, the price that could be commanded in the second context would be significantly higher, not only in the economic context of supply and demand, but because of the usefulness and benefit, the value, of the water to our survival in that situation. We'll explore the distinction between price and cost in more detail in Chapter 7.

Understanding value is crucial for improving how we negotiate and what we achieve from it. It's important to remember that our core (intrinsic) value as people doesn't change, even though others might see us as more or less valuable depending on what they need at the time. This means our value to others (extrinsic) can change based on their current needs and interests.

Knowing this helps us to not doubt our own worth, but to confidently own it. For example, if a company makes you redundant, it's usually because their needs have changed, not because your personal value has diminished. I've seen friends struggle with their self-confidence after being let go, not realising that it was the company's needs that changed, not their own intrinsic value as individuals. They are still just as valuable as they were before.

I know through my own life and career how much these skills have developed me as a person, how they have developed my strategic and business capability, my understanding of human behaviour and how to protect myself from being exploited by others who carry a different moral compass. But more than anything, they've helped me to get out of my own head, know my value and be more confident in asking for what I want. The conversation with my pesky voice is better managed, and as a result, I am less likely to avoid leaving value sitting on the table undiscovered.

The high cost of not negotiating

I dread to think how much money I've left 'on the table' over the years. I'm not just talking about commercial business deals, I'm talking salary offers, salary increases, bonuses, mortgage rates, store discounts, rentals, buying and selling houses, and all the other occasions I failed to ask for what I wanted because I didn't want to feel the discomfort of 'negotiating' a better deal. Subconsciously, I didn't want to shatter the belief I had formed that it wasn't possible to get what I wanted. Upon reflection, I realise that belief was to justify my avoidance of negotiating. Is this true for you? Can you think of one or more times you missed out or could have negotiated a better outcome but were too afraid or unsure of how to approach it? If your answer is 'yes', this book will help that become a thing of the past.

I started my career in finance as a management accountant, so you'd expect I'd have realised the compounding effect of not negotiating sooner, and therefore avoided the massive loss of the cumulative financial benefits over time, but I didn't. I didn't connect the dots quickly enough that each time I *didn't* ask for a raise or I accepted the measly inflationary increase without challenging it, that it wasn't just the few thousand in salary I didn't get and the interest I'd have accumulated on the extra cash that I missed out on, it was the compounding effect of every future percentage salary increase being calculated on a lower base. I didn't account for the reduction in pension/superannuation contributions that were also a percentage of my salary. Those decisions to not ask didn't just cost me then, they're still costing me now, and they'll continue to cost me into the future. Perhaps you're starting to see how a choice about your salary now, when you consider the compound effect of the reduced salary, interest and superannuation contributions over the years, will impact the amount you'll have available for your retirement. I think of how much more there could have been if only I hadn't avoided negotiating. If you've made, or are making, the same choices I once did, then we'll work on how you can make the change now so you can maximise the things that are valuable to you.

Compound interest calculator

It's confronting to see how much money you can lose if you choose not to negotiate. To give you a real example, let's say you negotiated a $15 000 increase in salary. If you invested that money in a low interest savings account each year, it could be worth over $1.1 million in 30 years and it could be worth even more with other investment options. This is what it could look like.

Initial deposit:	$15 000
Interest rate:	3% yearly
Time:	30 years
Deposits:	$15 000 yearly (at end)
Deposit increase:	3% yearly
Compounding:	Monthly
Total after 30 years:	$1 103 540.74

Use an online calculator to punch in some numbers to see how negotiation skills could propel your financial position forward.

When I look back, I realise I was subconsciously choosing the minimum acceptable standard to me. In all my negotiations, I chose comfort over discomfort and told myself stories like:

- it's probably not possible to get what I want

- if it were available, they would automatically give me more

- it's not worth risking looking foolish by asking for what I want.

I accepted the minimum standard of not believing in myself and not believing in my ability to get more value. I was in my own head negotiating with myself, and I had no idea that I had negotiated myself down to a minimum standard that was less than what was available.

Misconceptions about negotiation

Negotiation is very misunderstood. I'm always surprised by the variety of answers I get during training sessions when I ask participants to share what comes to mind when I say the word *negotiation*. I notice their eyes as they look around the room wondering who's going to answer first, and the short pause before the first person hesitantly answers: *win-lose, win-win, conflict, tactics,* etc. There is a palpable sense of relief at the end when I reveal that their answers aren't wrong, that each adds a different perspective to how we experience negotiation and what we understand it to be. So, what comes to your mind when you think of negotiation?

During my years of teaching negotiation skills to corporate leaders, I've realised just how often the art and science of negotiation is misunderstood, and why so many people don't achieve the outcomes they hope for. At business networking events or social gatherings, the most common question I'm asked is: 'What do you do?' This often reveals a significant gap between what people think I do as a negotiation specialist and the actual nature of negotiation.

Many people imagine that negotiation is all about high-stakes scenarios, like big boardroom business deals or intense conflict situations. Even among professionals, there's a widespread belief that negotiation is about using outdated tactics, such as strategic power plays, manipulative mind games or aggressive bargaining. But, in reality, negotiation is much more nuanced and collaborative than most people think.

Negotiation is part of everyday life

Fundamentally, *negotiation is a conversation to reach agreement.* It's something most of us do every day without realising we're negotiating, and yet, surprisingly, it's a skill many, including some of the most powerful leaders in the world, fail to master.

Before I began teaching negotiation skills to others, I didn't see how universally applicable negotiation is in everyday life and how necessary negotiation skills are to a successful life. Our understanding of negotiation is often limited to specific contexts, such as buying and selling in business, de-escalation during hostage situations, and resolving conflict in legal disputes. Because we don't consciously, or even unconsciously, connect negotiating with everyday conversations, we fail to consider the many benefits of being better at it. Perhaps you're ready to accept the first step that *every* conversation to reach an agreement is a negotiation.

Let's take today for instance—what negotiations have you completed?

- *Deciding on a movie:* Did you negotiate with a friend or family member about which movie to watch, finding a compromise that suits both tastes?

- *Meal choices:* Maybe you negotiated with your partner about what to have for dinner, balancing each of your culinary tastes to decide on a meal that works for both of you?

- *Work tasks:* You might have negotiated with a colleague over who takes responsibility for the tasks on a project, ensuring that the workload is fairly distributed?

- *Kids' bedtimes:* If you have children, negotiating bedtime can often be a challenge. Perhaps today you negotiated reading one less story? Or the children negotiated one more story (more likely!).

- *Social plans:* Maybe you negotiated with friends about where to meet for coffee or which park to go for a walk in after considering the different preferences and schedules?

By making this conscious connection, we can recognise that these everyday interactions are, at their core, negotiations. In doing so, it highlights how valuable being better at negotiating is, not just in high-stakes business or legal scenarios, but in our regular daily communications as well.

Even if, at heart, we understand that negotiation is simply a conversation to reach agreement, there is a reason most of us will fail to get good at it. Why? Because the key distinction between an effective negotiation and a regular conversation is *intention*. It's intentionally preparing:

what	we say and do
when	we say and do it
where	we say and do it, understanding
why	we're saying and doing it
how	we say and do it
who	we say and do it with
which	is the best approach to saying and doing it!

Every conversation where you're seeking to get agreement requires intention. Whether it's with your romantic partner, children, family members, friends, colleagues, customers, suppliers, investors or other stakeholders, it's the absence of this intention that sees more of those conversations fail to get the agreements they could.

Before you can begin to be intentional with others in conversations to reach agreements, you need to first be intentional with the daily conversations you have with yourself.

Negotiation starts within

As I stare at the blank page, with the cursor flashing on the screen, the negotiation with myself has already begun. The pesky little voice in my head is already challenging me: 'OK, you know a lot about negotiation—you've been doing it and teaching it for years, but what do you know about writing a business book? How are you going to bring value to the reader like you do in training sessions? What were you thinking when you signed up to do this?' This pesky voice isn't just living in my head, I've learned, it's living in yours too. What doubts, fears and negative self-talk do you tell yourself on a daily basis?

These inner conversations are common to all of us; we're negotiating with ourselves daily. Whether it's about applying for that next promotion, going on a date with someone new, taking the lead sales role on a big customer deal or seeking investment in your business, we're going to hear that pesky little voice.

I had a client recently share with me: 'We're just a mum-and-pop business. How are we going to negotiate the successful sale of our business with a world-leading company?' Now that's not a strong position in which to enter a negotiation, is it?

Like many of us, I thought that voice lived only in my head. It was only when I started working with others, first as an executive coach and then as a negotiation specialist, that I got confirmation that this pesky negative voice is within all of us. The question is, are you going to turn this pesky voice into an ally? Will you reframe it as an opportunity to be better or let it rule your life? My client promised never to refer to their business as a mum-and-pop operation again. This was step one on the path to creating value and building the foundation for a successful negotiation and sale.

At some point or another, we all question ourselves, our value and our worthiness, but it's not always so obvious that's what we're doing. The inner negotiation we have with our pesky voice can sometimes be masked as the voice of reason; it's the voice that keeps us safe from the fear of rejection, the fear of judgement or the fear of being exposed for not feeling good enough.

Oprah said it best when she spoke, reflecting on the thousands of interviews she has conducted over the years:

I came away with the understanding that the thread that runs through all of human experience is that we all want to be validated ... And the most you can ever do for somebody is to show up and allow them to know they have been seen and heard by you.

Deep down, we're really questioning, 'Do I matter to me?' It's this awareness of our human need to be valued that helps me understand the most common mistake I see being made in a negotiation—being in our own heads and having conversations with our pesky inner voice.

We lose ourselves in our own discomfort, we travel down rabbit holes with questions about our own abilities, and we doubt our worth. By being in our own heads, we consequently fail to consider the needs of the other person and fail to view our contribution, and therefore value, in the context of those needs. All those times Mum asked me to negotiate for better value on her behalf, I didn't once consider how valuable my English-speaking, -reading and -writing skills were to her. Growing up in India, she'd never had the privilege of education, yet she was working so hard to provide access to education for me and my sister. Instead, I focused on avoiding looking foolish and was lost in my own discomfort. I failed to see the value I could have brought to the table—even then, as an amateur teenage negotiator.

The conversation I want us to intentionally have in this book is one about your intrinsic value and your worthiness. I want you to be intentional about who you can become and what you can achieve through the power of effective negotiation. This conversation is crucial because each of us holds unique value, often unrecognised, as we overlook who could benefit from what we offer. We wait for external validation instead of proactively considering what others might find valuable, and in which contexts our contributions are most meaningful. Effective negotiation is about identifying the value others seek and recognising how and when the unique value we bring becomes significant.

You may still struggle with this inner voice that doesn't hesitate to highlight your deepest insecurities. Over the years, I've developed effective practises to quiet my own doubts and silence my pesky voice when it starts making a ruckus. I doubt there's any specialist who doesn't at one time or another doubt themselves — negotiation specialists aren't always immune to this pesky voice of doubt either. The difference lies in the intention with which we engage with, and move beyond, our internal dialogue to move towards success.

Are you ready to be intentional with the conversation you're having with yourself?

Avoid misguided pursuits of validation

I specifically remember one client telling me that she had to 'earn the right' to have a baby. She feared her career would go backwards if she didn't first prove her value to the business. Her pesky voice was telling her she needed to work harder and longer to secure her position before she could allow herself to get pregnant. When the time eventually came where she felt she'd done 'enough', the long hours and the extra stress that weighed heavily on her mind affected her body's ability to conceive, and it took her several years before she eventually had a baby.

She didn't negotiate a better solution for herself (and her manager) before doubling down at work. It was unthinkable that she could have a conversation about what she needed. She was caught in the spiral of doom in her own head, negotiating with herself and questioning her own value. She made assumptions about her work environment that may have been untrue and based on her unvalidated assumptions. She made decisions about her time and energy that nobody had asked her to make, which caused significant harm to her wellbeing.

She unconsciously avoided negotiating with her manager and, as a result, failed to maximise the value that she could have gotten for herself and the value she could have given others—she didn't know what was most important to her manager because she simply didn't ask. Sadly, stories like this aren't uncommon. Can you think of an example at home or work where you've failed to ask the necessary questions? It's important that we are intentional with the conversations we have with ourselves and the agreements we're making with our pesky voice. By getting out of our own heads and getting into others' heads, we shift our focus from our internal doubts and assumptions to understanding the perspectives and needs of those around us. By doing so, we can more consciously choose how to bring our value to the table, ensuring that it is both relevant and appropriate.

We negotiate to grow personally

During my two decades in the corporate world, I've learned that, at heart, we all want to be valued and to know we are of value to others in return. Today, I'm better equipped to hear what's not being said and to interpret what is being communicated even when words are not spoken. My interactions with others have deepened because my awareness has heightened and my confidence in both myself and my ability to achieve high-value outcomes has grown exponentially. This is why I'm writing this book—to help you build confidence in yourself and in the value you bring, both for yourself and your business. Negotiation skills open up opportunities for creativity, connection, curiosity, compassion, care and contribution. If you've noticed, that's a lot of Cs—maybe it's a sign that we should Cs the day and fully embrace these values!

In today's world, a world that continues to experience wars and conflict, there is a greater need for collaboration over competition. A need for connection over division. A need for creativity not rigid rules. A need for value creation over value distribution or, worse, value destruction. We are surrounded by challenges, but by focusing on these critical Cs, we can navigate our way towards a more cooperative and fulfilling global community.

The challenge that exists for all of us is the decision we must make about who we are, because negotiation isn't simply something we do, it's an extension of who we become in the process. Like money, negotiation skills can be used for harm and self-orientation or as a power used for good, where everyone's interests are considered.

Why master the art and science of negotiation?

Perhaps you're concerned that developing these skills might require you to be someone that you're not? Don't be concerned. I personally couldn't have anticipated that by being a better negotiator I would become a better person. I'm more compassionate, patient and caring. Don't confuse this with being soft. I care as much about results as I do relationships! But negotiation skills have given me a more powerful and effective way of getting those results. I bring curiosity to the conversation to create connection and I get to be creative with identifying solutions to problems. Just like water dripping for an extended period of time can cut through rock, I've learned it's the daily intentional conversations that we have consistently over time that have a huge beneficial impact on the results we get. We're using our skills to work smarter, not harder. What would your life be like if you could develop these skills?

This book is a personal call to action for you. An opportunity to lean into creating more value for yourself and the business you work for. But it's also a call to action to create a more connected and collaborative world. It's time for us to change the outdated images that are conjured up by negotiation from competition to collaboration, from win-lose to winning together, from communication manipulation to communication mastery. We all have value to give and it's our job to discover our own value and discover the value others have to give. It's only through discovering each other's value that we will be better able to exchange it. Maximising the value we each get can only be possible if we can first learn to identify it.

Negotiation changes the way we see the world

For a long time, in my naivety, I approached negotiation as if I were playing a sport where you either won or lost. I remember countless interactions with stakeholders where I failed to consider their needs and interests. I needed to be in control, to be right, to be smart. I was in a privileged position in the finance department with full visibility of the business's performance. My key stakeholders were across the various organisational functions, including sales, procurement, marketing, operations and supply chain. I was negotiating with seasoned negotiators, so for each negotiation I 'won', I fulfilled the deeper need within me to demonstrate my value to the business.

Instead of seeing the potential for teamwork, I viewed my colleagues from other departments as competitors. This mindset turned our regular commercial meetings from a training ground to build our collective team strength into more of a rivalry game.

During my years of experience working with teams across functional areas in large companies, I've noticed that it's easy for people to fall into these patterns. We often get so caught up in proving our own worth that we forget that real success comes from collaboration, from setting up plays together, passing the ball and scoring as a team. Perhaps you've observed similar dynamics at your workplace, where it seems like everyone is playing their own game instead of working together?

I first learned formal negotiation skills six years after finishing university. But back then, no-one really explained how these skills could change who you are, not just how you negotiate. I didn't fully grasp the concept of 'value'. I understood give and take, but I thought of it as just an arbitrary method to 'win' negotiations.

I also misunderstood what it meant to make a real contribution. I used to think contributing was just about giving something to others. It took me a while to realise that true contribution is more about the impact you create through your presence, attitude and approach, rather than just the actions you take during the negotiation process.

When negotiation is understood at its deepest level, it changes the way we see the world. Small interactions take on greater significance, and what begins as a hidden skill becomes a powerful, visible superpower. This transformation not only changes us as individuals, but also reshapes the landscape of our business and personal relationships, leaving a lasting impact on those we encounter.

Now that we've explored why negotiation is such a crucial skill for maximising and exchanging value, both personally and professionally, we'll explore which negotiator type you are. This will help you better understand how you can effectively apply the skills detailed in this book in your own life.

Negotiation nuggets:
Why we negotiate

- *To reach mutual agreements*: Negotiation is essential for coming to agreements in various aspects of life.

- *For purposeful communication*: Effective negotiation is intentional, setting it apart from regular conversation and ensuring more meaningful outcomes.

- *To avoid settling for less*: By engaging in negotiation, we prevent ourselves from accepting less than what we could potentially achieve.

- *To avoid long-term losses*: Not negotiating can lead to significant cumulative losses over time, which negotiation helps to prevent.

- *As a daily necessity*: Negotiation isn't just for special situations; it's a vital part of our everyday interactions.

- *To maximise and exchange value*: Through negotiation, we aim to enhance and share value, not just win or lose.

- *To recognise value*: Negotiation allows us to understand the importance, benefits, usefulness and worth of something to ourselves and others.

- *To fulfil a universal human need*: It addresses our inherent desire to feel valued and to value others.

- *To understand and express our worth*: Negotiation skills aid in articulating our own value and in recognising the value of others.

- *It's a transformative skill*: Negotiation has the power to change how we view and interact with the world, making it a crucial life skill.

Focus five action list: Why we negotiate

Action	Activity	Done
Identify your core values	Reflect on and write down your top three personal values to guide your negotiation priorities.	
Recognise everyday negotiations	Notice and acknowledge life's daily negotiations, such as deciding on chores at home or agreeing tasks with people at work, to practise and refine your skills.	
Set clear intentions	Before negotiating, clearly define your goals and consider the other party's perspective to approach the conversation strategically.	
Practise asking for what you want	In low-stakes situations, practise articulating your needs and desires to build confidence for bigger negotiations.	
Reflect on past negotiations	Think back to previous negotiations to understand what held you back and identify ways to improve for future negotiations.	

Chapter 2

Which negotiator type are you?

How well do you know your negotiation style? Negotiation is as much about knowing yourself as it is about understanding others. Start by completing the quiz at www.thevaluenegotiator.com/playbook and then read on to learn about the various negotiator archetypes. Understanding what kind of negotiator you are and the negotiation style of others you'll be negotiating with, both in your business and personal life, will put you in a strong position to succeed. This is also a great exercise to run with your team, so not only are they aware of their default archetype, but you gain an understanding of the mix of styles within the team and can use them to your business's benefit.

In this chapter, I'll introduce you to various negotiator archetypes: The General, The Diplomat, The Dealer, The Accommodator and The Avoider. These archetypes are adapted from the work of Kenneth W. Thomas and Ralph H. Kilmann, who developed the Thomas-Kilmann Conflict Mode Instrument (TKI) in the 1970s. This model was introduced to help individuals and groups understand and assess their behaviour in conflict situations and measure how assertive vs cooperative they are in reaching resolution. In the negotiation context, we'll look at this through the lens of valuing outcomes vs relationships (see figure 2.1).

The aim here isn't just to label your negotiation style, but to help you grasp the practical implications of your inherent approach. It's about understanding the strengths and potential pitfalls of your style. Knowing your style is important, but learning how to adapt to or complement the styles of others is just as crucial. A word of caution with these archetypes: they are guides, not rigid categories. Negotiation is complex, and it's unrealistic to box people into a single type that explains all their behaviour, especially when their stress response is activated. While you may find you have a default/preferred archetype, under stress you might find yourself automatically switching archetypes. Also, once you are aware of these archetypes you can begin to consciously choose which archetype to adopt based on the context and your assessment of the most appropriate behavioural approach.

Use these archetypes to understand general trends and themes, this allows you to flex your style to suit various situations. Remember, when you negotiate, you're dealing with real people, not just faceless companies. In business, decisions usually aren't made by one person alone. Often, if you misunderstand the different archetypes that may be involved, you might find deals falling apart as they go through different levels of approval. It's important to understand the different styles of everyone involved on both sides. This is much easier, of course, when you know the other party and have had previous dealings with them. In situations where the other party is unknown, use the matrix in figure 2.1 to ascertain whether they appear to be more concerned about the relationship or the outcome to give you a starting reference point.

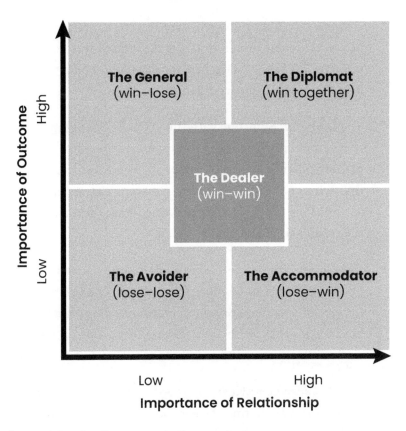

Figure 2.1   the five negotiating archetypes

What's your negotiator type?

Are you someone who prioritises relationships or outcomes? When you consider your negotiator type, I want you to think about your default approach and please be honest with yourself—you won't get what you need from this if you hide behind the lens of the profile type you wish you had. In your negotiations, where you place the importance of relationships and outcomes, on a scale from low to high, will determine your negotiator type.

- *The General:* Winning is what matters most, getting their desired outcome even if it means the relationship isn't a priority. This style works best for situations where the result holds significant importance.

- *The Diplomat:* Someone with this style of negotiating aims to win together. Getting the best outcome possible for all without hurting the relationship. They look for solutions that achieve the desired results and keep relationships strong. This is a great approach when both the stakes and the relationships are highly valued.

- *The Dealer:* They focus on keeping things balanced in their pursuit of win-win, comfortable with compromise they aim for agreements that are an acceptable middle ground for both the results and the relationship. This style is chosen when both aspects are somewhat important, but not critical.

- *The Accommodator:* Keeping a good relationship is more important than getting the best outcome. This yielding style is chosen when the relationship is more valuable than the specific issue at hand.

- *The Avoider:* The Avoider doesn't place much importance on either the outcome or the relationship. This style is used when the negotiation or conflict isn't considered worth the effort or if they are consciously seeking to delay conversations.

As you consider which negotiator type is most aligned with your default approach, read the corresponding section in this chapter to see what you need to consider. Also, think about who else comes to mind as you read the different types? Can you recognise the different negotiator types you experience at work and at home?

Making the unconscious conscious

To be an effective negotiator I had to first make my unconscious behavioural approach conscious. In different contexts and scenarios, both personally and professionally, I noticed my approach varied, depending on whether the outcome or relationship was the more dominant focus.

I learned that my default stress response is to fight rather than flight or freeze, so in the past, when triggered, I tended to default to give more importance to the outcome over the relationship. This often led me into the archetype of The General under stress, sometimes without realising it.

It was only after making this unconscious behaviour conscious that I recognised I had a choice in my approach. By developing my emotional intelligence, I was better able to regulate my emotions in stressful situations. Now, my go-to approach is The Diplomat, but when appropriate, I do use The General and The Dealer. The Diplomat is the most obvious archetype to aspire to because it's the behavioural approach best suited for high-value outcomes where the relationship is also highly important, but it is actually the hardest to emulate in practise.

I found this to also be true with the participants attending my workshops. Many of them often believe they are the collaborative Diplomat archetype, but under pressure, they see how challenging it is to maintain the relationship while also seeking to optimise the value in a deal. In a workshop environment, they are recorded negotiating, and we play back and analyse their behaviour so they can learn what happens to them under pressure. What we believe about our capabilities in a rational state doesn't always align with what happens in a high-pressured emotional state.

Negotiation is not a skill you can simply read about and expect to master immediately. It requires you to consciously practise your skills and to become an observer of what's happening, so you can choose the most appropriate behavioural response.

In this chapter, there is further detail of what you will see in each archetype along with their associated strengths and things to watch out for. I've also included a guidance section, so you know how best to navigate moving forward.

The General

Generals are all about capturing as much value as possible for themselves. They are tough and assertive, often putting their own goals ahead of everything else. They strive to win and are not afraid to use aggressive tactics to get what they want, even if it means the other person loses out.

Generals are not shy about using their power and authority to get their way; they're competitive and rarely back down from an opportunity. This is great in situations where you want to secure a high-value contract; however, this style is known as a 'win-lose' approach in negotiation. The General sees negotiation as a competition to be won, and their strength in advocating for the company's interests must be tempered with input from other team members to avoid damaging long-term business relationships.

If you see yourself as a General in negotiations, you are likely to be bold and driven. You know how to push for what you want and are not afraid to make tough decisions quickly. This can be a great asset as it allows you to advocate strongly for your interests and take charge of negotiation situations.

However, it's important to be aware of the potential downsides. Being focused on winning at all costs can sometimes damage relationships in the long run, which might be harmful if you need to collaborate with the same people again in the future. Additionally, being too assertive might lead to resistance from others, making it harder to achieve your goals if people feel pushed into a corner.

Strengths

- The General is great at standing up for what they want. This means they can push hard to meet their goals and make sure others know what they're aiming for.

- They make decisions fast and stick by them. This can really help in negotiations where being quick and confident is rewarded.

- They have a strong presence. People notice them when they walk into a room, and they can often use this to their advantage to lead discussions.

Things to watch out for

- Because they focus so much on what they want to achieve, they might not pay enough attention to the relationships they're building (or breaking) along the way. The people they negotiate with today might be the ones they need tomorrow.

- If they push too hard, especially when they're not in a strong position, it might backfire and people could push back or resist.

- Sometimes, focusing on getting a quick win can make The General miss out on better opportunities that take longer to develop.

Guidance for The General

- *Build bridges:* Always try to build and maintain good relationships during negotiations. Try to find things you and the other person agree on as much as possible. This can make negotiations smoother and more successful.

- *Think ahead:* Don't just focus on the here and now. Sometimes, working together or finding a middle ground can be better than trying to win at all costs. Think about how your decisions affect future opportunities.

- *Use your strengths wisely:* You have a strong personality and you're good at being firm—that's great, but use these traits wisely. It's not always about being the most dominant person in the room; sometimes, being strategic about when to assert yourself can have a bigger impact.

- *Stay open to change:* Your way isn't the only way. Some people might react negatively to a very aggressive style. Listen to feedback and be willing to adjust your approach if needed.

The Diplomat

Diplomats default to creating value that benefits all parties involved. They prioritise building strong relationships and finding common ground. Open communication, active listening and collaboration are key to their approach. Diplomats aim for outcomes where everyone wins because they believe that mutual success fosters better long-term cooperation.

Diplomats combine assertiveness with empathy, carefully balancing their own needs with the interests of others. They are good at understanding different perspectives, which helps them unlock new value for all parties during negotiations. This style is a 'win together' approach because it focuses on collaboration, making sure everyone comes out ahead.

In long-term contracts, where tricky price increase conversations must be had, The Diplomat excels because of their ability to build and maintain trust in relationships and create mutual value.

If you identify as a Diplomat in negotiations, your strengths likely include your ability to collaborate, paired with an assertiveness to get the most optimal result. Your aim is to build strong relationships, find common ground, and work towards mutually satisfying outcomes through creating and growing value together.

However, there are challenges to this approach as well. In some scenarios, a purely collaborative approach may not yield the best results. Also, an excessive focus on maintaining relationships might sometimes lead to under-asserting your own needs, which could be counterproductive in certain negotiations.

Strengths

- The Diplomat is collaborative, cooperative and focused on building relationships. This helps them create agreements that everyone feels good about.

- They emphasise active listening and empathy, and understand other people's needs and perspectives, which can lead to more effective solutions.

- They can assert their own needs and interests when necessary. They know how to stand up for what they want without being confrontational.

- Diplomats are good at building value. They know how to make negotiations beneficial for all parties involved.

Things to watch out for

- Value creation may not always be possible. Sometimes, the ideal win together scenario isn't achievable.

- They might naively assume that the counterparty has the same interest in creating value as they do. Remember, not everyone comes to the table with the same collaborative intent.

- While balancing assertiveness with empathy is a strength, there can be instances where their assertiveness might be perceived as overpowering. This could potentially intimidate or alienate some people.

- In their enthusiasm for finding solutions, they may sometimes overshadow other voices. They need to ensure that all parties have the opportunity to contribute.

- An excessive focus on maintaining relationships might lead to under-asserting their own needs, which could be counterproductive in certain negotiations.

Guidance for The Diplomat

- *Set clear boundaries:* While your collaborative nature is a strength, it's important to establish clear boundaries to ensure your needs are met. Practise assertiveness in a way that respects both your needs and those of others.

- *Be realistic about intentions:* Understand that not everyone shares your collaborative mindset. Assess the intentions of the other party realistically and be prepared to adapt your approach if they are more competitive or self-serving.

- *Encourage inclusive dialogue:* Use your skills in active listening and empathy to facilitate inclusive discussions. Make sure all voices are heard and avoid dominating conversations, even in your enthusiasm to find solutions.

- *Be prepared to walk away:* You naturally look for creative solutions that benefit both parties, but recognise not everyone has the will or skill to do this. Balance empathy with strategic thinking and be willing to walk away if the other party is not willing to negotiate in good faith.

The Dealer

Dealers default to sharing value, achieving mutually acceptable outcomes through a balance of give and take in negotiation. They value fairness and compromise, recognising that sometimes both parties may need to make concessions. This approach is rooted in a strong negotiation skill set, but focused on aiming for middle-ground solutions that benefit both parties.

Dealers are excellent communicators and listeners, and are good at finding common ground and fostering balance. Their negotiation style can be described as compromising; it is all about flexibility and the strategic exchange of value. Think of scenarios like budget negotiations where compromise is necessary, finding solutions that meet most of the company's needs without over-extending resources.

If you see yourself as a Dealer in negotiations, you likely appreciate the importance of flexibility and creativity in reaching solutions that are fair for everyone involved. You might find satisfaction in outcomes where no party feels disadvantaged. However, the compromising nature of a Dealer also has its pitfalls. The willingness to balance interests and split the difference can sometimes result in others taking advantage of your reasonable nature.

Strengths

- Dealers can make necessary concessions to reach an agreement, valuing flexibility and the ability to compromise.

- Their creativity and problem-solving skills help devise solutions that satisfy all parties.

- They strive for progressive outcomes, focusing on the overall benefits of the negotiation.

Things to watch out for

- Dealers may compromise more than necessary, potentially diluting the optimal outcomes.

- Their strong sense of fairness could be challenged if others do not share their balanced approach.

- Prioritising getting a deal over maximising value can sometimes lead to less favourable outcomes.

- Being perceived as accommodating may impact their negotiation leverage and credibility.

Guidance for The Dealer

- *Avoid default compromise:* Don't automatically settle for a middle-ground solution; strive to achieve the best outcome for all involved. Focus on maximising the benefits rather than just evenly splitting them.

- *Leverage problem-solving abilities:* Use your strong problem-solving skills to develop innovative solutions that provide added value. Ensure that any compromises are strategic and benefit both sides equally.

- *Clear communication:* Always articulate your needs and interests clearly during negotiations to ensure they are fully considered and understood by all parties.

- *Stay flexible and ready:* Keep an open mind to all possible solutions and be ready to walk away from the negotiation table if the proposed terms are not beneficial.

- *Expand the pie:* Aim to increase the total value available through negotiation (grow the pie), rather than just dividing what is already there. True fairness in negotiation comes from creating outcomes where everyone feels they have gained something valuable. Imagine you and your colleague are negotiating your responsibilities for a shared project. Instead of simply splitting the tasks 50/50 (dividing the pie), you discuss your individual strengths and interests. You thrive in client communication while your colleague is great at data analysis. By aligning your responsibilities with your strengths and proposing new ideas to improve the project, you create a more efficient workflow and better outcomes. Both of you gain something valuable and expand the pie by increasing the value of the project.

The Accommodator

Accommodators are known for giving value, adopting a generous approach in negotiations and always looking to make the other person happy, even if it means making personal sacrifices. They focus on the long term, often prioritising relationships over immediate gains. Their approach can be summed up as 'if you're happy, I'm happy'. They embody the 'accommodating' negotiation style, which is all about ensuring the other party's satisfaction.

If you align with The Accommodator's way of negotiating, you probably place a lot of importance on the needs and happiness of others, sometimes even more than your own. You prefer to avoid conflicts and strive for peace, believing that maintaining good relationships is more important than winning any single negotiation. This focus on harmony and empathy can foster strong bonds and positive interactions; however, there's a risk that others might take advantage of your accommodating nature.

Strengths

- Accommodators are motivated by maintaining harmony and therefore more willing to yield their position rather than prioritise self-interest.

- Their empathetic listening and trust-building skills help create and maintain strong relationships.

- They are viewed as friendly and approachable, which can make people more comfortable in negotiations.

Things to watch out for

- Accommodators might compromise too much, which could lead to them not fulfilling their own needs.

- Avoiding necessary confrontations or tough decisions might prevent them from achieving the best outcomes for themself.

- Others may underestimate them in more competitive or business-focused settings.

- Constantly putting others first may eventually wear them down.

Guidance for The Accommodator

- *Balance giving and receiving:* While nurturing and maintaining positive relationships is important, ensure that your own needs are also met. Aim for agreements that benefit both parties, not just the other side.

- *Look to the future:* Consider the long-term effects of your accommodating nature. While it's important to be cooperative, also think about how your tendencies to over-give might affect future negotiations. The current concessions you make need to be appropriately balanced with the potential for future interactions.

- *Leverage your empathy:* Your strong suit is your ability to empathise and connect with others on a personal level. Use this skill wisely. Being empathetic doesn't always mean you have to give in to others' demands; sometimes, it means understanding enough to find a mutually beneficial solution without short-changing your own needs.

- *Stay adaptable:* Keep an open mind about your negotiation style. Being overly accommodating can sometimes lead to being taken advantage of. Be prepared to adjust your approach if the situation calls for a firmer stance or if being too agreeable isn't yielding the best results.

- *Develop assertiveness:* Practise expressing your needs and standing up for your interests in a respectful manner. Building assertiveness can help ensure that your voice is heard, and negotiations are more balanced.

The Avoidant

The Avoidant's default is to protect value. They prefer to steer clear of conflict, prioritising comfort and peace over potential gains from confrontation. They tend to protect their current state and avoid situations that might lead to stress or disagreements, often choosing to withdraw or delay dealing with issues. This approach is based on a defensive negotiation style, focusing more on preventing losses than chasing potential wins.

In situations such high-tension board meetings or family arguments, Avoidants are great at not being drawn into the conflict. They are good at side-stepping issues until a more appropriate time. However, they don't often follow up on dealing with the issues that must eventually be addressed to avoid any detrimental impacts on the business and relationship.

If you resonate with the Avoidant style, you likely try to minimise conflict whenever possible. You might delay discussions or hope problems will resolve on their own to maintain peace, even if it means not advocating for your own interests as strongly as you could.

This method of avoiding conflict can be protective, but also limiting. By not engaging in timely negotiations, you might miss opportunities to address and resolve issues beneficially. Avoidants focus on dodging difficulties rather than seizing opportunities to advance.

Strengths

- Avoidants are good at maintaining peace and avoiding stress for themself and others.

- Their empathetic nature helps them understand and respect other people's feelings.

- They prioritise others' comfort, sometimes even above their own needs.

Things to watch out for

- Avoidants may avoid issues too long, causing unresolved conflicts or built-up resentment.

- By steering clear of confrontations, they could miss chances to create value or improve situations.

- There is a risk of them becoming overly cautious and imagining worse-case scenarios.

Guidance for The Avoidant

- *Seek engagement:* Rather than withdrawing from negotiations, try to stay engaged, even when it feels uncomfortable. Look for ways to gently confront issues rather than avoid them. This can lead to more effective resolutions and prevent problems from escalating.

- *Consider long-term impacts:* Don't just focus on avoiding conflict in the moment. Think about how avoiding issues might affect your relationships and opportunities in the future. Sometimes, addressing problems directly can lead to better outcomes down the line.

- *Use discretion:* You naturally avoid conflict, which can be a useful trait; however, use this trait wisely. It's not always about avoiding every confrontation; sometimes, carefully choosing which conflicts to address can improve your position and relationships.

- *Embrace flexibility:* Remember that your comfort in avoiding conflicts isn't always the best approach. Be open to adapting your style when necessary. Some situations may require you to step out of your comfort zone and tackle issues head on to achieve the best results.

Dealing with the different archetypes

Understanding the negotiation style of your counterpart can significantly influence the outcome of your discussions. By adapting your approach to align with their style, you can navigate negotiations more effectively. Below are specific strategies for dealing with each archetype.

Dealing with a General

When negotiating with a General, it's wise to let them think they are winning. You can achieve this by creating an illusion of compromise, making it appear as if you are giving in on minor points, so they feel like they are getting their way. Additionally:

- *Prepare thoroughly:* Generals respect strength and knowledge. Have your facts, data and rationale ready.

- *Be assertive but not aggressive:* Match their confidence without being confrontational.

- *Find common goals:* Empathise mutual benefits and long-term gains to align their competitive nature with cooperative outcomes.

Dealing with a Diplomat

Building trust is crucial when interacting with a Diplomat. They value transparency and mutual benefits. Strategies include:

- *Share your needs clearly:* Be open about what you want and why it matters to you. Diplomats respect people who can express their needs honestly while also being considerate of others' needs.

- *Ask questions:* Engage in active listening and encourage them to share their perspectives.

- *Collaborate on solutions:* Work together to explore options that create value for both parties, emphasising mutual success and long-term relationships.

Dealing with a Dealer

Dealers appreciate fairness and balance. When negotiating with them:

- *Base your arguments on logic and fairness:* Present well-reasoned arguments that highlight equitable outcomes.

- *Be prepared with options:* Offer multiple solutions to facilitate a perceived equitable exchange.

- *Highlight compromises:* Emphasise the fairness of the proposed solutions and how both sides benefit.

Dealing with an Accommodator

Accommodators prioritise relationships and harmony. To negotiate effectively with them:

- *Express your concerns:* Whether genuine or strategic, share your concerns to prompt them to proactively seek solutions.

- *Support their needs:* Ensure their needs are addressed to foster goodwill.

- *Encourage mutual benefits:* While they may prioritise your needs, remind them of the importance of their own interests for a balanced outcome.

Dealing with an Avoider

Avoiders steer clear of conflict and may delay decision-making. Strategies include:

- *Use a gentle approach:* Avoid aggressive tactics that may push them further away.

- *Highlight consequences:* Show them that avoiding a decision could lead to worse outcomes and encourage them to engage.

- *Offer reassurance:* Provide a safe space for discussion and emphasise the importance of addressing issues constructively.

Negotiator types in team dynamics

'If only you thought and acted more like me, then we'd get on!' We often wish people would align more with our expectations, thinking that life would be easier if others looked and behaved as we wanted them to. The reality is, whether we're negotiating at work or at home, we're inevitably faced with people who are different to us.

Negotiating one-on-one is challenging enough, but the dynamics become even more complex when negotiating as a team, whether that's in a complex commercial business deal or organising family travel plans. When we understand these five archetypes, we can recognise the different approaches our team or family members might take in reaching agreements.

While it's natural to judge one style as better than another, it's more helpful to consider the various archetypes in different settings. At home, the accommodating nature of your partner allowing you choose what movie you both watch could be a blessing, but if you're seeking their input on a decision and they respond with, 'I'm happy with whatever makes you happy', it might cause you frustration.

However, being aware of their style will help you understand how to leverage their strengths and mitigate their vulnerabilities, and the same is true for those we work with. In this case, appreciate your partner's flexibility and willingness to support your choices and encourage them to express their preference by saying, 'I value your opinion and really want to make a decision that we both feel good about, can you share what you think would be best?' This helps ensure their input is considered and leads to a more balanced and satisfactory decision for both of you. Have you ever had a line manager who is constantly seeking to please stakeholders and yet can't make a decision for the good of their own team's interests? That's an Accommodator.

Choose your team based on objectives

When you're considering the appropriate archetype to use amidst team and family dynamics, keep in mind the objectives of the negotiation. For example, in a business negotiation for a one-off transaction where preserving the relationship isn't paramount, The General's assertiveness could be key. On the other hand, when negotiating family matters, like planning a family holiday, where maintaining harmony is essential, The Diplomat's skills are invaluable.

Balance is important in any team composition, be it at home or at work. Pairing different archetypes, like The General with The Diplomat, can bring both assertiveness and empathy to the table, covering a broad spectrum of approaches. This is as helpful in boardroom negotiations as it is in family discussions about important financial decisions.

Communication and adaptability is crucial

In your professional team, ensure everyone is clear about the collective strategy and how each archetype contributes. Similarly, in your family negotiations, being open and clear can prevent misunderstandings and help each family member understand the other's viewpoint.

Sometimes you need to adapt to the style of those you're negotiating with. In business, if you're facing an aggressive counterpart, The General's approach might be effective. In personal situations, like resolving conflicts with relatives, an approach more like The Diplomat's may be beneficial. It's not easy to switch your default approach, especially under pressure. Begin by identifying friends, family or colleagues who you think fit each archetype, and then practise different approaches as if you were imitating them. What would they do in the same situation? It makes it much more real and easier to relate to when you have someone in mind rather than just the archetype alone.

Be mindful of the dynamics in your team or family. Dominant personalities should not overshadow the more accommodating ones—sometimes you need to create space for your Accommodators or your Avoidants to be heard. Create an environment where everyone, from the assertive to the peacekeepers, can express their perspectives.

Consciously consider the versatility of your skills in handling different scenarios. Adapt by understanding and utilising each archetype according to the situation, whether this is you borrowing the skills of another archetype or leveraging the talents within your team. This enables you to use your collective strengths to reach more valuable outcomes.

Who are you being?

In this chapter we've looked at the different behavioural approaches and considered the situational contexts in which they may be appropriate. For me, however, a crucial element in the development of our negotiation skills, and our growth at a more philosophical level, is reflecting on the questions: *Who am I being and who do I aspire to become?*

For much of my career, I viewed skill development as a path to achievement, performance and success. But what I've learned is that an even more potent measure of a journey isn't just our achievements, but the identity we embrace.

Knowing who we aim to become anchors the skills we develop and the intention with which we apply ourselves. Through many missteps in my life, like the time I tried to emulate a colleague's avoidant negotiation style only to realise it conflicted with my intrinsic values, I recognised that the most powerful agreements we first have to make are with ourselves.

Have you had a moment when you felt out of sync with your values during a negotiation. How did it affect the outcome? How did it make you feel about the process and yourself? We can't control how others perceive us, but we can control our character. If we are intentional about who we're being and who we aspire to become, then the agreements we make with others will naturally reflect our values and the contribution we aim to make.

In each of my two businesses, The Value Negotiator and Heart of Human, I'm reminded of the essence of the identity I've chosen. To be The Value Negotiator, I must first identify the value that others seek and then align it with the value that I have to exchange. The focus on *value* reminds me that it's what we *value* in life that ultimately drives us.

Living in a capitalist society, we are often surrounded by notions of greed and scarcity. Recognising our need to feel valued and understanding that we have the choice to contribute positively allows us to navigate this environment more thoughtfully. We can choose to be creators of value, rather than participants in value destruction. As demonstrated by the different archetypes, how we choose to behave is ultimately derived from what we value.

As we continue to the next chapter and learn what to consider in negotiation, remember that the most impactful negotiators are those who know themselves deeply. They negotiate not just for immediate gains, but for outcomes that resonate with their values and enhance their relationships. By embracing who you aspire to become, you can transform not only your negotiation outcomes, but also how you contribute to the world around you.

Negotiation nuggets:
Which negotiator type are you?

- *Understand your style*: Begin by identifying your natural negotiation style through a self-assessment at www .thevaluenegotiator.com/playbook. Understanding whether you prioritise relationships or outcomes helps you navigate both personal and business negotiations more effectively.

- *Recognise negotiator archetypes*:

  - **The General:** Focuses on winning, often at the expense of relationships.

  - **The Diplomat:** Aims for mutually beneficial outcomes, preserving relationships.

  - **The Dealer:** Seeks balanced compromises, maintaining some focus on both results and relationships.

  - **The Accommodator:** Prioritises relationships over outcomes, often making personal sacrifices.

  - **The Avoider:** Typically disengages from negotiation to avoid conflict altogether.

- *Adapt and complement styles*: Being able to adapt your style to complement others in negotiations will enhance outcomes and relationship dynamics.

- *Use each style's strengths*: Each negotiator type has unique strengths; use these effectively to improve your negotiation outcomes.

  - **The General:** Assertiveness and quick decision-making.

- **The Diplomat:** Collaboration and value creation.

- **The Dealer:** Creativity in compromise.

- **The Accommodator:** Empathy and trust-building.

- **The Avoider:** Maintaining peace and avoiding premature confrontations.

- *Anticipate and manage pitfalls*: Be aware of the potential downsides of each style to avoid common pitfalls in negotiations.

  - **The General:** Might damage long-term relationships.

  - **The Diplomat:** May struggle in highly competitive situations.

  - **The Dealer:** Could be seen as too accommodating.

  - **The Accommodator:** Risk of being exploited.

  - **The Avoider:** Possible missed opportunities due to non-engagement.

- *Strategic guidance for each type*: Leverage your negotiation strengths and mitigate your vulnerabilities.

  - **The General:** Build bridges and think ahead to prevent relationship damage.

  - **The Diplomat:** Balance assertiveness with collaboration.

  - **The Dealer:** Aim for the best outcome, not just a compromise.

- **The Accommodator:** Ensure personal needs are also met.

- **The Avoider:** Engage more directly to avoid missing out.

- *Reflect on personal growth and choices*: Consider how your negotiation style aligns with your personal values and long-term goals. Reflect on 'Who am I being, and who do I aspire to become?' to solidify your identity and negotiation approach.

Focus five action list: Which negotiator type are you?

Action	Activity	Done
Take the quiz	Complete the negotiation style quiz at www.thevaluenegotiator.com/playbook to identify your default negotiation archetype.	
Reflect on your style	Consider how your default negotiation style affects your outcomes and relationships. Write down examples of when your style has been beneficial and when it has been a drawback.	
Observe others	Pay attention to the negotiation styles of people you interact with. Identify their archetypes and note how they handle negotiations.	
Adapt your approach	Practise adapting your negotiation style to fit different situations and counterparties. For example, try being more diplomatic in a high-stakes negotiation or more assertive when the outcome is critical.	
Team exercise	Run the negotiation style quiz with your team. Discuss the mix of styles within the team and strategise how to leverage these styles for the benefit of your business.	

Chapter 3

What to consider in negotiation

'I didn't even know you could negotiate that!' It still surprises and saddens me how often I hear this. Whether it be from clients, friends or new acquaintances, I see their moment of revelation as they begin to recognise the unexplored potential they have in negotiating.

Until I started teaching negotiation skills to others, I had no idea how others perceived negotiating and to what extent they leveraged it in their lives. It's easy to make a flippant statement like 'everything is negotiable', but the reality is, we don't experience life that way. So much of what we want can feel impossible and out of reach. Our negotiations are often confined within invisible boundaries set by tradition, perceived norms and our past experiences.

While it's true that some goals might be out of reach, my aim here is to expand your thinking and approach to negotiation. There is so much we don't even think is negotiable, and I want to help by sharing why broadening our scope is so impactful and then help you cultivate a mindset that uncovers and seizes hidden opportunities.

My hope is that this chapter shows you that it is more than just learning to negotiate differently; it's about transforming the way you think about and approach every aspect of negotiation in your life.

What's negotiable?

Given that we know that negotiation is a conversation to reach an agreement, you can imagine the endless opportunities we have to negotiate if we approach each conversation with that intention. Some of the most obvious examples include those in the following areas.

Our personal life

- *Salaries and job benefits:* Salary, bonuses, paid holidays, remote working options

- *Real estate:* Purchase prices, agent commission, finance terms, settlement dates

- *Relationships:* Where to live, whether to buy or rent, when or if you get married, whether you have children

- *Big purchases:* Cars, home appliances, furniture

- *Services:* Fees for services, such financial planning, legal work, medical treatments, home improvement projects, utilities, mobile phone.

Business

- *Service contracts with customers:* Terms, prices, service levels

- *Pricing:* Bulk pricing, rebates, recurring customer discounts, early payment discounts, fixed/variable terms

- *Partnerships:* Equity splits, revenue sharing, roles, responsibilities

- *Key performance indicators:* Revenue, profit and working capital targets, year-on-year growth percentage

- *Supply agreements:* Terms for supply, including price, quantity, delivery specifics, payment terms.

Everyday situations

- *Credit cards:* Interest rates, repayment terms, penalties

- *Insurance premiums:* Coverage details, premium amounts, claim conditions

- *Rental agreements:* Lease length, monthly rates, clauses (like pet policies), deposit amount, exit clean requirements

- *Negotiations with ourselves:* Commitments to personal and professional goals, time management

- *Interpersonal negotiations:* Where to go for dinner, what movie to watch, home chore allocation, etc.

The scope of what can be negotiated is so broad that it surprises me that we aren't taught these skills earlier and that we aren't made aware of different contexts in which we can benefit from applying these core skills. With each opportunity we have to negotiate, we have to consider what we want and why we want it. Not everything that can be negotiated should be negotiated; sometimes the reward just doesn't match the time, energy and effort required; for example, negotiating a refund of a late payment fee on your credit card when it takes over an hour to get through to a customer service representative might not be worth your time and effort. So consciously choosing what not to negotiate is as important as choosing what to negotiate. The key distinction here is that our decision must be made consciously.

What gets in the way of discovering what's negotiable?

It would be great if we were all given a comprehensive list of everything that is negotiable. However, life doesn't work that way, and even though there is an abundance of opportunity, much of what's available to be negotiated is never discovered. This happens for a number of reasons that stem from a lack of:

- *Knowledge:* We don't know what can be negotiated so it limits the scope of what we do.

- *Flexible thinking:* We can be rigid in our thinking, which stops us looking for creative ways to get better outcomes.

- *Effective communication:* We don't always listen as well as we could or ask the questions that could help us discover more of what's available.

- *Confidence:* We don't always back ourselves to propose something different or explore alternative options.

- *Conflict resolution skills:* We fear having difficult conversations, which leads us to avoid important negotiation points.

- *Curiosity:* We make assumptions that something isn't negotiable, so we don't find out if there is scope.

- *Time:* We don't plan for our conversations intentionally, so we rush conversations, leaving us little room to explore more opportunities.

- *Relationship building:* We don't build the depth of connection, the lack of which prevents people opening up and revealing their deeper needs and interests to us.

- *Focus on non-price factors:* We make it all about money and so we don't think about negotiating for other things that could be valuable.

- *Preparation:* We don't make the time to research and explore what could be available, so we limit ourselves based on our past experiences.

You may even identify other reasons why you haven't discovered what's negotiable, but what I find helpful to acknowledge is that all of the ones listed here are within our control to change. The challenge we often have is that we can't change what we can't see. So, we have to consciously begin to consider what might be holding us back.

Case study: What time is check-in?

I once attended a business retreat in Uluru, the red centre of Australia. As I joined the queue for the hotel check-in with other fellow female business owners, we encountered an unexpected opportunity to negotiate. The first person from our group approached the counter and was informed that the hotel had allocated a time for the members of the business retreat to be checked in and, because it was two hours in advance of that time, she'd have to come back later. As she exited the line, I overheard her passing the same message on to other members of the group in the queue. Some pulled out of the line and others

(continued)

stayed. As each one of them went to the different counters, they provided their details only to be told the same thing.

As I arrived at the counter, I was asked if I was part of a group booking. I confidently said 'no'. While I was attending the retreat, I hadn't booked my accommodation as part of any group booking. We had all booked our accommodation independently. The lady behind the counter found my details and informed me that, as I was noted to be attending the retreat and was therefore part of the group, that I'd have to come back. I was prepared for this because of what the others had experienced. In a calm, yet assertive tone, I proceeded to ask if she could first check if my allocated room was ready. She paused, a little surprised by my question. I maintained my expectant gaze, and upon checking the system, she informed me that it was. I smiled and responded with: 'That's wonderful. So you won't mind checking me in?' A few moments later I was checked in and heading out of reception with my room key. The remaining ladies in the queue followed my lead.

This situation showed me the practical side of negotiating: getting small, everyday agreements. I had used my understanding of negotiation to read the situation, and explored what might be possible. What negotiation skills have taught me is that there is always opportunity to make the ask and that we'll never get 100 per cent of what we want if we begin by settling for less.

How many times have you accepted a 'no' or a 'later' without question? Can you think of a situation where a bit more assertiveness or a simple question could have changed the outcome? Sometimes, it's these small outcomes that we get that can teach us the most about how we approach opportunities and whether we uncover the possibilities that are available.

What do you believe is negotiable?

Much of our assessment of opportunities is influenced by what we believe is negotiable, and too often we're bound by rules or policies that we don't question. In the example I shared of the business retreat, the hotel's rule was to check in the group at a certain time—I imagine so as not to clog the check-in counter for other non-business retreat guests and so they could manage the group together. But, it also didn't make sense to me why the receptionists were sticking to their arbitrary allocated check-in time when it became apparent that they were duplicating their efforts by checking details of each guest to confirm if they were part of the group attending the business retreat and turning them away even though rooms were ready.

It's interesting how many people don't question rules. It's not always possible to change the rules, and I'm not suggesting rules aren't appropriate, but in a negotiation situation, it is important that we question them. If we blindly accept rules, then we may leave value on the table.

The rules we make up in our own minds, otherwise known as our own beliefs, can also be a significant block to us discovering what is negotiable.

One of the most powerful processes I've found to question whether what I believe is accurate is a set of questions developed by Byron Katie, an American speaker and author who teaches a method of self-enquiry that she calls 'The Work'. I use this method to help me unpack my beliefs in day-to-day life, as well as to help me with discovering what's negotiable.

The Work is centred around four questions:

- Is it true?

- Can you absolutely be 100 per cent certain that it's true?

- How do you react when you believe that thought?

- Who would you be without the thought?

Let's take these questions and apply them to the common belief that you may have that 'This is not negotiable'. These four questions can be used as a litmus test to challenge your own thinking around a situation and whether it is as rigid as you believe. Think of a situation where you would typically assume there is no room for negotiation. Let's take the example of negotiating a reduction on your home loan interest rate.

Is it true that this is not negotiable?

Only answer the question with a 'yes' or 'no'. You may initially feel very certain about your response.

Can you absolutely be 100 per cent certain that it is true?

This question encourages you to go a level deeper through reflection. Can you absolutely be certain that it is a situation that is completely non-negotiable? Are you 100 per cent certain that no-one in the world has ever negotiated in this situation? If we take our example of negotiating a reduction in our home loan interest rate, we might consider that, even if we've never negotiated a reduction, we can't be certain no-one in the world has.

How do you react when you believe that thought?

When you believe the thought your home loan interest rate is non-negotiable, notice what emotional and behavioural response you experience. Do you feel stressed, frustrated by the belief or powerless? Does it give you closure to the discussion? Does it give you a sense of rigidity and stop you from asking?

Who would you be without the thought?

What behaviour would you see in yourself if you didn't believe that it wasn't negotiable? Would you be more open, flexible or willing to explore alternatives? Would you make the phone call more readily to your bank? Would you call other banks and find out what your options are?

This is a powerful exercise that I've used many times. It works because it plants a small seed of doubt into what could be a fixed mindset around a situation. What usually happens next ultimately depends on whether we water that seed of doubt, and allow ourselves to explore new possibilities, or choose to stay fixed with our original beliefs—our own made-up rules that may limit us.

I know from personal experience that it can feel very uncomfortable to think that we may be leaving value on the table, but, as I mentioned, we can't change what we can't see. We must look with intention.

What behavioural approach do you need in negotiation?

When it comes to negotiation, it's natural that we find ourselves leaning towards our preferred approach to negotiation, which is either competitive (e.g. The General) or collaborative (e.g. The Diplomat). Most of my clients tend to believe that they lean towards collaborative approaches until I show them how easily they default to being competitive. What's important is that we're not wedded to just one way of doing things. Being effective at negotiation means being able to switch between both styles when the situation calls for it. Knowing when to be competitive and when to be collaborative with others will significantly improve your negotiation outcomes. In Part Two of this book, I'll give you further clarity on how you can determine which behavioural strategy is appropriate when. For now, I want you to consciously acknowledge what these behavioural approaches entail and why these different behavioural approaches are necessary.

Competitive behaviour

Competitive behaviour involves focusing on your own interests, often with less concern for the other party. If you picture a cake, your goal is to secure as much of it as possible, sometimes at the expense of others—a challenge The General would readily rise to meet. When you are competing, you are essentially claiming or capturing value, which typically means what you get is what the other party gives up. It's a win-lose approach that might mean having to leverage the other party's weaknesses to your advantage.

Competing = Claiming or capturing value

Collaborative behaviour

In contrast, collaborative behaviour is about jointly finding solutions that benefit everyone. It's not just about claiming or capturing value for yourself, it's about creating a situation where both parties benefit—something that The Diplomat strives for. In this situation you can imagine you're working together to bake a larger cake. Instead of competing for slices of an existing cake, you're making a bigger one together, so that there's more to share between you. When you collaborate, you have the opportunity to create value through joint effort.

Collaborating = Creating value

The dilemma that will always present itself is that, even when you bake a bigger cake, you will still have to determine how you will share it between you, and splitting it squarely down the middle, as The Dealer might, isn't always the most optimal outcome for all parties. If you identify as an Accommodator, you're likely to be collaborative but not creating value, instead giving value away. As an Avoider, your behaviour may be neutral, but could also be perceived as competitive or uncollaborative if it's delaying a decision or not engaging at all.

Creating and sharing value requires a high level of emotional intelligence where both parties are self-aware as well as other aware to avoid value being destroyed in the process of sharing it.

But what happens when your counterpart's approach to negotiation doesn't match your own?

Case study: Mel and Ed's business partnership

Mel was ready for a change when she decided to partner with Ed. After five years of running her business solo, she was excited about the idea of sharing the journey and aiming for joint success. Ed, a group CEO, approached Mel with a promising vision: by joining his network of businesses, Mel would enjoy the camaraderie of a team while retaining her independence. Ed painted a picture of growth and wealth increase for Mel through referrals and a stake in the larger business group.

However, within six months, Mel's optimism turned to dismay. She realised that Ed's promises didn't quite match reality.

(continued)

Ed was eager for Mel to share her client database for cross-selling purposes across the group, a detail he hadn't mentioned before. He also expected her to share her personal assistant, funded by her business, with other group members. Additionally, as her business had the best cash flow, Mel found herself unexpectedly funding another director's salary.

Mel had approached this partnership collaboratively, hoping for mutual benefit, but soon saw that Ed and the other directors had a competitive agenda. They were using her business as a stepping stone for the group's growth, rather than seeking a true partnership, as Mel had envisioned.

When Mel approached Ed about dissolving the ill-aligned partnership, she maintained her collaborative approach, believing Ed would understand her perspective and see the unfairness. Instead, Ed cut off communication and accused her of breaching their agreement.

In her search for a resolution, Mel came to me still hoping for a collaborative solution; however, I pointed out that her approach wasn't suitable given Ed's self-serving tactics. Ed was demonstrating the behaviours of The General archetype, while Mel was adopting The Accommodator archetype, focusing too heavily on the relationship and yielding to Ed's needs while she was being adversely financially impacted. It was clear that Mel needed to adopt a more competitive stance to protect her interests.

Reluctantly she shifted her approach towards The General archetype: she stopped trying to preserve the relationship, matched his transactional communication approach on email and engaged a lawyer to legally present her proposal with clear consequences and deadlines, and successfully dissolved the partnership. While she couldn't recoup all her losses, this strategic shift in approach prevented her being further exploited and saved her business from potential ruin.

This experience taught Mel a valuable lesson: while collaboration is ideal, understanding when to switch to a more self-protective, competitive strategy is crucial, especially when dealing with partners who prioritise their own gains above mutual benefit.

Time to check in with yourself

- *Self-reflect on your approach:* In your past negotiations, have you leaned more towards a collaborative or competitive approach? Reflect on a specific instance and consider whether a different approach might have led to a better outcome.

- *Recognise others' behaviours:* Think about a time when you were in a negotiation. Were you able to recognise whether the other party was being more competitive or collaborative? How did that recognition (or lack of it) affect your strategy?

- *Identify red flags:* Reflecting on Mel's experience, can you identify any red flags from your past negotiations that indicated a misalignment in approaches or intentions? How might you more effectively spot these signals in the future?

- *Consider adapting your strategy:* Have you ever found yourself in a situation like Mel, where the other party's actions didn't align with your expectations? How did you respond? Could you have adapted your strategy to better protect your interests?

- *Learn from experience:* Considering Mel's shift from a collaborative to a competitive approach, can you think of a similar adjustment you've made or could make in your negotiations? What lessons did you learn or could you learn from making such an adjustment?

We need to get creative with levers

There is so much that can be learned from negotiating, not least that in every situation there are many levers and variables that can be negotiated. Levers are the elements in the negotiation that can be flexed; they're ultimately what we give and take on to reach an agreement. The more we negotiate, the more we learn how many different elements of the agreements we make are negotiable.

If we take an example of a home renovation, what levers would you negotiate? Here some of the negotiation levers could include:

- *Budget (price):* You can negotiate a lower total cost by comparing quotes and using the lowest bid to leverage better offers from others; for example, 'I've received several quotes, and while I prefer your work, your quote is the highest. Can we discuss ways to reduce the cost to match or come closer to the other quotes?'

- *Scope of work:* You can define or redefine what renovations are necessary to manage costs and essential needs; for example, 'If we focus on essential upgrades in the kitchen now and leave the cosmetic changes for later, could that adjust the overall price?'

- *Quality of materials:* You choose between different quality of materials to balance costs and durability; for example,

'I want a durable countertop because it's a high-use area, but I'm open to less expensive tiles for the backsplash. Can we explore some cost-effective options there?'

- *Timing and scheduling:* You can negotiate a start date and duration of the project; for example, 'If I allow you to start the project during your slow period in early winter, could we negotiate a lower overall cost?'

How many more did you identify? There are so many different variables we can leverage to get the agreement that we want. The more levers we can identify, the more opportunity there is to work collaboratively and create value. When there are only a small number of levers available, it means that there are fewer elements we can flex on in a deal to create an acceptable agreement. This can also mean that there is greater chance of each party taking a competitive approach to claim or capture value. When there are fewer levers, there is usually less opportunity to get creative and create more valuable solutions.

With the levers we identify, it's important to prioritise what matters most, and to whom, and be willing to make concessions on areas that are less important so that we gain on the ones that are most important to us.

What does effectively using levers involve?

- *Understanding your own priorities:* Know what's important to you and what you're okay with giving up.

- *Finding out the other party's priorities and pressures:* Figure out what the other person in the negotiation really cares about or might be worried about to help you create more valuable proposals.

- *Creatively combining different levers:* Think of all the things you can negotiate on (like price, payment terms, scheduling etc.) and try to come up with a deal that would benefit both parties.

- *Making a strategic concession:* Sometimes you have to give up something to get something else that's more important to you.

Understanding levers and how to use them effectively does more than just help us get better outcomes, it shifts how we approach negotiations. It allows us to get creative with identifying levers — the things that either we want or that the other party wants. It encourages us to listen and pay attention to the needs of others so that we understand what may be of value to them when considering the proposals we put together. It also helps us prioritise what matters, so we know how to exchange value effectively.

In the next chapter we'll look at who matters in negotiation, so you know who to take into account when you are considering the levers available to negotiate.

Negotiation nuggets:
What to consider in negotiation

- *What's negotiable?* Almost everything can be negotiated in both personal and professional contexts. The opportunities are infinite. We don't have to negotiate everything, but we must consciously choose what we will and won't negotiate so we don't blindly leave value on the table.

- *What gets in the way?* We can't change what we can't see. Identify the reasons you don't negotiate, such as lack of knowledge, rigid thinking etc., so you can navigate and remove these obstacles.

- *What do you believe?* Use self-enquiry methods like Byron Katie's The Work to assess your beliefs about what is negotiable. Remember beliefs are our own made-up rules — feel free to change them if they don't work for you.

- *What behavioural approach do you need?* Both competitive and collaborative approaches are necessary in different contexts and which one you use depends on whether you're trying to create value or capture value.

- *What happens when your counterpart's approach doesn't match your own?* Adapt your strategy, leveraging both competitive and collaborative approaches as the situation demands.

- *What can we learn from negotiating?* Get creative with identifying levers. Levers give you more options to flex the deal and find a mutually beneficial solution. The more levers, the more ways you have to explore solutions.

Focus five action list: What to consider in negotiation

Action	Activity	Done
Identify negotiable areas	Make a list of aspects in your personal and professional life where you can negotiate, such as salaries, service contracts and everyday purchases. This will help you recognise more opportunities to negotiate.	
Challenge your beliefs	Use Byron Katie's four questions to challenge your assumptions about what is negotiable. Reflect on a specific situation where you think negotiation isn't possible and apply these questions to it.	
Observe and learn from small negotiations	Pay attention to everyday situations where you do negotiate, like asking for a better service or more favourable terms. Reflect on these small wins to build your confidence.	
Prepare and research	Before entering any negotiation, thoroughly research what is negotiable. Understand the other party's needs and priorities to identify potential levers you can use.	
Get creative with levers	Identify multiple negotiation levers, such as budget, timing and scope of work. Think creatively about how you can combine these levers to reach mutually beneficial agreements.	

Chapter 4

Who matters in negotiation

In negotiation, understanding the *who* is as important as the *why*. Time and again, I've witnessed people fail to understand who they're negotiating with because they are solely focused on getting the outcome they want. This has led to compromised deals or, worse, them being exploited. If we don't take the time to consider who matters in our negotiations, we have to accept that it's a significant oversight that can change the whole outcome.

Negotiation is everywhere, yet, ironically, many of us don't see the need for developing these skills, as evidenced by the disproportionate amount of our time we spend in disagreements or navigating interpersonal politics. Take a moment and think about how much time you are regularly spending navigating disagreements or differences of opinions at home and work? This paradox highlights the critical need we have for enhancing our communication skills, which, as a core outcome of effective negotiation skills, is often overlooked.

Today, our world seems more inclined towards anger and outrage than curiosity about others' perspectives. We only need to spend a few moments on social media to see how challenging it is for many of us to consider perspectives that are unique and different from our own. A global lack of curiosity prevents us from understanding different viewpoints, this, in turn, hinders our ability to negotiate effectively and create solutions that are beneficial for everyone. It's only through intentionally getting curious about others that we can navigate conflicts more effectively and reach agreements in a more collaborative way. Sadly, we're witnessing a world where even global political leaders' resort to initiating wars and conflicts, a stark reminder that even some of the world's most powerful leaders haven't developed the curiosity needed to explore agreements that benefit everyone.

The simple and unpopular truth is that we're too focused on our own interests and needs. We're so consumed with what we want that we're neglecting to consider the perspectives and needs of others. This self-centric approach doesn't just make it hard to reach good agreements; it stops us from building strong, lasting relationships, which is core to successful negotiations.

The acceleration of advances in technology is increasing the curiosity and critical thinking gap and slowing our evolution of human emotional intelligence. While our technology gets smarter, our ability to empathise, understand and negotiate with fellow humans doesn't keep pace. You may have noticed, in many areas of business and life, our interactions are becoming more transactional. We spend more time with our heads in our phone or looking at computer screens and less time being present and really getting to know one another. Navigating a world where we have sophisticated technology at our fingertips, but often lack the fundamental human skill of effective communication is a huge problem. We're creating a societal shortfall where we're equipped with efficiency tools, but are not so good at connecting with people or dealing with emotions and complex negotiation situations.

This is why we'll explore why it's essential to not just identify, but thoroughly understand who's involved in your negotiations. It's not just about reaching an agreement, it's about creating solutions that work well and satisfy all parties. When we extend our focus beyond our own immediate needs and wants, we can create opportunities for more comprehensive, inclusive and satisfactory outcomes. Through understanding who matters, we have the opportunity to create a better world for all of us.

Who's at the table?

Drawing from my own experience during two decades of collaboration with executives in large global corporates, I've come to the conclusion that we're not very good at identifying who's at the table or who needs to be. Sure, we can say we're busy, but we can't ignore the fact that we have more resources today than ever to facilitate efficiency, yet we still seem to lack the time for intentional thinking prior to our conversations to ensure that we understand who the interested parties are and what they care about in our pursuit of an agreement.

This lack of intention often means we overlook key people, leading to missed opportunities and potential conflicts. In the rush of our tech-driven lives, we're working harder but not necessarily smarter. This fast-paced environment makes it challenging to be thorough in our negotiations and to really consider the needs and perspectives of everyone involved.

In this chapter, I'll show you how to identify the various parties that may be involved in your negotiations. You'll learn about their roles, interests and how they shape the negotiation landscape as well as why they matter to us.

Meet your Joker

In every negotiation training workshop, I find a common theme: people negotiate with themselves. It's that pesky voice inside your head that you often don't prepare to deal with and who is actually a big part of your negotiating team.

When you're negotiating with yourself, how do you know which voice is the real you? One voice is your Joker, the emotional wild card of your ego. It can be animated, loud and demanding, worrying about what others think and how things will affect your image or future. The Joker is the part of you that attaches your identity, your sense of self, to things like your social status, your different roles in life, your job, how much money you make, your life experiences and what you own or wish to have.

Professor Steve Peters talks about this in his book *The Chimp Paradox*, where he calls our emotional side, the ego, our Chimp. Both the Chimp and the Joker are the parts of our brain that can help us, but also make things difficult, especially when we're under stress. They can take over our logical thinking with emotional reactions. Whether you think of this part of your brain as a Chimp or a Joker, understanding it is key to handling how your emotions affect your decisions, especially in tense situations.

On the other hand, your 'Authentic Conscious Expression' (ACE) is quiet and calm. Unlike the Joker who is always focused on 'doing' something, your ACE is more about just 'being' in the moment, watching things unfold. This part of you doesn't tie your worth to your job or what you own; it just observes your thoughts and actions without getting too wrapped up in them.

When people say they feel like they're negotiating with themselves, I understand that they're struggling with their Joker. It's the pressure talking, with their Joker worrying about the future. But when they use their ACE, they start seeing things more clearly, stepping back to observe calmly. Recognising this and moving from impulsive quick reactions to thoughtful responses is a core change in how they approach negotiations.

Our aim shouldn't be to shut up our Joker, but to understand and control it. It's about knowing it's there, using its strengths, but not letting it run the show. The Joker can give us useful instincts, such as for creative problem-solving and personal safety, but it should be balanced by the calm, rational ACE for making good decisions. When you next notice your emotional Joker taking over, imagine being in the control room of your mind, and pressing a large yellow button labelled 'Calm' that you can use to gain immediate control over your emotional self. Pressing this button makes your Joker disappear for a while, so you can think clearly without its emotional interference. At times, when you've been emotionally hijacked, focusing on your breath can also gently redirect your energy from the urgent emotional Joker to the calm ACE.

Before we explore who else is at the negotiation table, remember that you're always dealing with these two parts of yourself. Understanding how to balance your impulsive emotional Joker and your rational ACE can really improve your negotiation skills. Choosing the right 'card' to play, whether it's the Joker or the ACE, will help

you handle discussions better, bringing the best version of yourself to every negotiation.

Who are you negotiating with?

There are various names for the person, group or entity that you are directly negotiating with. I refer to them as your 'primary counterpart' in the negotiation process. Some will refer to your counterpart as your opponent or opposition, but words carry meaning, and calling them your opposition already paints a clear picture of your expectations of the other party and may influence your approach in dealing with them. When it comes to your counterparts, recognise that their interests and needs may be aligned, opposed or neutral to your own. Therefore, understanding their motivations, limitations and objectives is crucial.

What's also important to remember is that if there are 'two' of you, then there are 'two' of them as well. If your Joker can show up as an uninvited guest at the table, it's likely theirs will too. You might think you know who your counterpart is, but you also need to understand who they become when their Joker steps out of its deck and takes a seat at the table. If we only anticipate our counterpart's needs when they are being their ACE, we fail to plan for the emotional reactions of their Joker. In preparing for a negotiation, we often make the mistake of expecting ourselves and others to be logical and rational, but the reality is that negotiations are highly emotional, and our Jokers often take a seat at the table with us.

How many times have you had a conversation that you expected to go smoothly, only to have it take an unexpected turn? If we don't recognise that each party is bringing two parts of themselves, we're setting ourselves up for failure before we've even started. In Part II, I'll discuss how to handle your internal Joker and predict the other party's reactions in more detail. I'll also give you specific strategies and techniques to effectively recognise and manage not just your own emotional responses, but also those of the person you're negotiating with. This way, you can approach every negotiation with a balanced and strategic mindset.

Who are you really negotiating with?

Sometimes the person we think we're negotiating with isn't the person we're negotiating with. If we take the simple example of house auctions, as prospective buyers, we are put in an environment where we're led to believe that we're negotiating against our competition, which in this case, are other prospective buyers. From our perspective, these other bidders represent the most immediate and visible 'competitors'. They are the ones with whom we are directly vying for the property, and their bids have a direct impact on our chances of securing the home.

During the bidding process at the auction, the tension and competition between these parties is palpable, which is why we perceive them as the primary counterparts. Meanwhile, the sales agents are circling around us, whispering in our ears, turning up the volume of our emotional Joker inside our heads. The agents often intentionally dial up our emotional drivers to encourage us to 'win' rather than 'lose' to our 'competition'.

However, what most of us fail to recognise is that, when it comes to buying and selling, it's not the competition we are directly negotiating with—it's the sales agents and the auctioneers on behalf of the sellers. They are the professional negotiators in this scenario who often orchestrate the auction and employ strategies to maximise the sale price. They hold key information about the seller's expectations and are skilled in managing the auction process. In terms of negotiation dynamics, they are a critical counterpart whose actions and motivations significantly impact outcomes.

The other prospective buyers, while we may perceive them as the other party we're negotiating with, are likely to also be used as pawns in a process, to drive up the price, when ultimately the seller and the sales agents are the primary beneficiaries.

This doesn't just happen in house auctions: tender processes also create the same competitive energy between businesses submitting tenders. Submissions focus on trying to be better than the competition, the 'perceived other party', but meanwhile, it's the hosts of the tender who create and control the conditions of the negotiation, and who are the party you're negotiating with.

So, what should you do:

- Gather as much information as possible about your counterpart.

- Understand their background, negotiation style, past dealings and objectives.

- Establish a baseline understanding of their ACE prior to entering a negotiation, otherwise you may find it harder to identify early signs that their Joker is emerging.

- Develop your negotiation strategy with the other party's likely reactions, preferences and goals in mind.

Who else matters? For each of the following examples, I want you to remember that these roles can be part of your *and* your counterpart's team. So, when you're thinking about how best to prepare for your negotiation, don't forget to consider who else is involved from both sides.

Who does the buck stop with?

Decision-makers have ultimate authority. They are people or groups who have the final say in whether a negotiation is successful. They are the ones who approve, reject or modify the terms of an agreement. Decision-makers often set the strategic direction and parameters within which the negotiation takes place, defining what outcomes are acceptable.

It's important to understand who the decision-makers are in the context of your negotiation. This could be your CEO, board of directors, the head of a family, or even a group of individuals with collective decision-making power. In many cases, especially in corporate settings, while senior executives may handle the day-to-day discussions, the final agreement usually requires approval from higher-ups.

For example, when negotiating a major contract with another company, the decision-maker might be the CEO, the head of procurement or sales, or an internal committee. Preparing for the negotiation involves understanding their business objectives, pain points and decision-making criteria. We need to research their goals, priorities and constraints. What drives their decisions? and What outcomes are they seeking? We'll cover more on this in Chapter 8.

Shape your negotiation strategy to align with the decision-makers' interests and priorities. Consider how your proposals will meet their needs and address their concerns. When it comes to your next negotiation, if you don't know if you're talking to the decision-maker, ask your counterparty: 'Besides you, who else will be making the decision?' Always find out who the buck stops with.

Who's influencing the outcome?

Influencers are people who have influence but don't have authority. They are the people who indirectly impact the negotiation process and outcomes. They might not be directly involved in negotiations, but their opinions, actions or positions can significantly sway the decisions and strategies of the negotiating parties. These influencers might be individuals within either organisation or even external parties, such as from the media, public opinion or industry thought leaders who can sway the negotiation indirectly.

For example, if you're in a company negotiating a merger with another firm, a key influencer could be a well-respected industry analyst whose opinions are highly regarded. Although not directly involved in the negotiation, their public comments on the merger can significantly sway shareholder opinions and affect the market perception of the deal.

Positive commentary from the analyst could increase shareholder confidence, leading to a smoother negotiation process with more favourable terms. Conversely, scepticism from the analyst could create doubts, potentially stalling negotiations or leading to more stringent terms from the other firm.

Influencers in this situation could also be competitor firms whose actions might influence strategic decisions and the positioning of the merger. For example, if another company is threatened by the potential merger of two competitors, they may engage with regulatory bodies and lobby for a review of the proposed merger due to anti-competitive concerns, which would, at the very least, delay the merger process.

In another everyday scenario, you're a parent pushing for changes in the school's extracurricular activities, and the issue is up for discussion at an upcoming PTA meeting. A prominent influencer in this situation is another parent who is not on the PTA but is known for their active involvement in school activities and who has strong relationships with other parents and teachers.

This parent's opinions are highly respected within the parent community. If this influential parent supports the proposed changes, their endorsement could create a favourable opinion among other parents, increasing the likelihood of the proposal being accepted at the PTA meeting. Their support might also encourage teachers to view the changes positively. On the other hand, if they express reservations or oppose the changes, it could lead to other parents and possibly teachers resisting the proposal, impacting the negotiation's outcome.

In places like schools, influential people are those who, because of their involvement and relationships, can informally affect what the group decides. It's really important to understand who these influencers are, especially in situations where getting everyone to agree is key.

These examples show that influencers, whether in business or personal settings, can have a big effect on negotiations without being directly involved. Their power comes from their expertise, the respect they command or their connections. Knowing, and maybe even working with, these influencers can be a smart move in negotiating.

Why does this matter? If you don't think about influencers, you might miss chances for support, run into surprise problems or weaken your negotiating position. Not considering them could also harm relationships and make it harder to put into action what's been agreed upon.

Who's bearing the impact?

The impact bearers are affected parties who, while not directly involved in the negotiation, will feel the impact of its outcome. Understanding their needs and perspectives is important because they can significantly influence the negotiation dynamics, even if they aren't at the negotiating table. They often serve as informal influencers. Their opinions, needs and reactions can sway the priorities and strategies of the actual negotiators.

This might include end-users, communities or even the environment, depending on the context of the negotiation. These impact bearers need to be considered in negotiations where the outcomes of negotiations have wide-reaching implications, such as organisational policy changes around gender pay transparency; community housing projects; or family decisions, like estate planning. In situations where decisions will have long-term effects, the input of the people who are affected is crucial for sustainable and acceptable outcomes.

In a corporate business acquisition, the impact bearers of the negotiation could include employees of both companies, shareholders and even customers. Preparing for negotiation in this context would involve understanding how each group will be affected by the acquisition, what concerns they might have (like job security for employees), and how this shapes your negotiation strategies.

By considering the needs of the impact bearers, we can ensure we've taken a more holistic approach to the negotiation, where decisions are made considering the broader impact, leading to more sustainable solutions and a higher likelihood of deal acceptance. As you think about your next negotiation, who will bear the impact of your negotiation outcomes?

Who's got a stake in the outcome?

Most people make the mistake of thinking that stakeholders are everyone who might be interested in the negotiation. Compared with influencers, a stakeholder's interest in the negotiation is more direct and personal and they have an active role in the negotiation process. While they may not have the final decision-making power, stakeholders have a vested interest in the outcome of the negotiation. They can be people within a company, such as employees, or outside it, such as customers.

Stakeholders are not neutral parties. Their concerns and interests are aligned with how the negotiation's outcomes will affect them or their group. Often, they have a more active role than the impact bearers. They may be involved in discussions, provide input or actively try to sway the negotiation to protect their interests. For example, in a negotiation for new payroll system, you may have procurement, IT, HR and finance all as key stakeholders.

Understanding who the stakeholders are and what they want is important in negotiations. Their needs and viewpoints can guide how the negotiation goes and what the goals are. Whether they agree or disagree with the proposed solutions can make a big difference in whether those solutions work out.

People who are stakeholders inside a company include employees, contractors, consultants and managers. They are a part of the company's daily life and success. Outside the company, stakeholders include customers, suppliers, partners, community groups or even government regulators. Their connection to the company is more about doing business with it or how it affects society.

It's expected that there will be overlap with some of the stakeholders you identify in the other categories listed. The key here is not to rigidly assign stakeholders to only one category, but to use these categories as a lens through which to identify and evaluate all parties that could be involved. Sometimes, using a different lens allows us to discover who might be actively involved in the process but was missed because they weren't a counterparty visible 'at the table'.

Who's providing expertise?

Advisers and experts in specific subjects can be helpful in negotiations because they know a lot about certain topics. They can explain complex or technical things, and they give advice on how to handle specific parts of the negotiation. This could be about legal clauses, money matters, technical details or things specific to an industry.

To illustrate: Sara was an employee who wanted to study more while working. She talked to a career coach to figure out how to balance studying with her job. She also checked with HR to learn about her company's rules for part-time work or educational leave. The coach helped her plan how to talk to her boss about the benefits of her studies, and the HR expert advised on how to fit her plan with company policies.

Or take Daljit, whose promotion meant moving to another city. He needed to negotiate a relocation package with his company. He got advice from a relocation expert about living costs in the new city and what's usually included in relocation packages. He also talked to a tax consultant about how moving would affect his taxes. This information helped him ask for the right things in his relocation package, such as moving costs, help with finding a house and adjustments for the cost of living. The tax consultant informed him about tax-deductible relocation expenses, which Daljit used to negotiate a tax-efficient package.

As an employee, it's likely that Daljit's company would have had access to these subject matter experts and so he may not have needed to seek independent guidance, but it's always important to verify that the subject matter expert is representing your best interests and ensure that there is no conflict of interest or bias.

If you're in negotiations involving complex legal, technical or industry-specific matters where specialised knowledge is required, determine which aspects of the negotiation might require specialised knowledge or technical insight. Integrate their insights into your negotiation strategy. This might involve preparing questions, understanding key issues or determining how their advice can shape your negotiation tactics.

Type of advisers and subject matter experts

So, I've emphasised the importance of consulting the experts to assist in your negotiation, but who exactly do we mean when we say 'experts'?

Legal advisers

Advisers are often involved in drafting, reviewing and advising on the legal aspects of the negotiation. Be aware that the approach legal experts often take (as opposed to commercial negotiation experts) is to negotiate on each individual clause in the contract. We'll cover more of this on page 243, but for now, understand that if you isolate and negotiate one clause at a time, you will not maximise the value available in the deal.

Technical experts

These experts have special knowledge about the topic you're negotiating. They can check whether what the other side is saying is correct and applicable, and give their own insights. Just be careful not to let them share more than you want them to in the negotiation itself, because subject matter experts often love to talk about their area of expertise!

Consultants

Whether from inside or outside your company, consultants can give advice on overall strategy, market conditions or negotiation tactics. As someone who consults on negotiations, I've helped businesses figure out how to handle things like price increases and complex deals. Don't forget, just because you haven't hired outside help, doesn't mean the other side hasn't sought external guidance.

Who's going to help if things go south?

This book is meant to help you make better agreements, but sometimes negotiations can be tough, especially when everyone's emotions (those Jokers) get involved. If negotiations hit a dead end or get really complicated, you might need a mediator or an arbitrator. It's important to know the difference between the two.

For instance, siblings James and Alexa were at odds regarding the care plan for their elderly father. Alexa wanted to hire professional in-home care, while James believed their father should move into an assisted living facility. A family counsellor with experience in elder care mediation was engaged as a mediator to help them find a solution.

The mediator conducted separate sessions with each sibling to understand their concerns and motivations. Alexa was worried about their father losing independence and the comfort of home, while James was concerned about safety and the need for the professional care available in a facility.

Through mediation, they realised their mutual concern was for their father's wellbeing. The mediator helped them explore a compromise where their father started with in-home care, with a plan to re-evaluate the situation periodically and consider assisted living if necessary. The plan also included regular family meetings to discuss and assess their father's ongoing care needs.

Arbitrators, on the other hand, often have specific expertise relevant to the dispute's subject matter. Unlike mediators, arbitrators listen to each party's argument and make binding decisions based on the evidence and arguments presented.

For example, Andrew was navigating a property boundary dispute with his neighbour. They couldn't agree, so they engaged a local land dispute arbitrator. The arbitrator examined the property deeds, land surveys and heard testimonies from both Andrew and his neighbour. The arbitrator then determined the correct boundary line based on the legal documents and land surveys, resolving the dispute with a clear, legally binding decision.

Mediators help find a middle ground through discussion, while arbitrators make legally binding decisions based on the facts.

Connecting the dots: Your stakeholder map

We've covered a lot because knowing *who* you are negotiating with is as important as understanding *why* you're negotiating. If we don't consider all the people involved, then we won't be prepared for the potential behavioural approaches they'll bring to the conversation. If we only focus on the outcomes we want, without considering who's involved, we'll only create suboptimal agreements because we aren't positioning our value effectively. Also, what's even worse is we could leave ourselves open to being exploited by parties we hadn't considered were involved in the process. By not considering who's involved, we fail to understand their motivations and the deeper interests they have behind the proposals that are made. Use table 4.1 to help synthesise the distinctions between each stakeholder type and create your own stakeholder map for your next negotiation.

In the next chapter, we move to explore when to negotiate, when not to and discover when time matters.

Table 4.1 stakeholder map

Stakeholder type	Role	Involvement	Influence	Key consideration	Notes
Joker (ego): self	Represents your emotional responses and fears	Always present internally	Can be high	Recognise when the Joker is influencing your decisions; practise mindfulness	Unique to self; involves managing your own emotions
Joker (ego): other party	Represents the emotional responses and fears of the other party	Present in other party's decision-making	Can be high	Anticipate emotional reactions from the other party; adapt communication accordingly	Consideration of the other party's emotional state and triggers
Other party	Primary counterpart in negotiation	Directly involved; key player on the opposite side	High	Research and understand their interests, goals and negotiation style	Clear distinction: the entity or person you are directly negotiating with
Decision-makers	Make final decisions on outcomes	Directly involved; ultimate authority	High	Identify their priorities and decision criteria	Can be both internal (e.g. company CEO) and external (e.g. regulatory bodies)
Influencers	Indirectly affect negotiations through opinion shaping	Not directly involved in decision-making	Moderate to high	Understand their impact on public opinion or specific groups	Can include both internal (e.g. respected employees) and external figures (e.g. media personalities)

(continued)

Table 4.1 (Continued)

Stakeholder type	Role	Involvement	Influence	Key consideration	Notes
The impact bearers	Impacted by outcomes, but not directly involved in decision-making	Indirect involvement: interests affected by outcomes	Moderate	Consider their needs and potential reactions to outcomes	Can include both internal (e.g. employees) and external parties (e.g. community members)
Stakeholders (internal/external)	Have vested interests in outcomes	Varies; can be directly or indirectly involved	Variable	Identify and understand their interests and influence levels	Stakeholders often span internal (e.g. employees, managers) and external (e.g. partners, suppliers) domains
Advisers/SMEs	Provide expert advice or knowledge	Consulted for specific issues	Moderate	Select for relevant expertise; balance their advice with overall goals	Primarily external, but can include internal experts within an organisation
Mediators/ arbitrators	Facilitate or decide outcomes in disputes	Brought in to resolve disputes or make binding decisions	High	Choose based on neutrality, expertise and reputation	Typically external, neutral parties

Negotiation nuggets:
Who matters in negotiation

- *Who's directly negotiating*: Focus on understanding the immediate negotiators, such as yourself and your primary counterpart.

- *Who's emotionally involved*: Acknowledge the emotional aspect in each of us, and the interplay between our emotional Joker and our ACE.

- *Who's the decision-maker*: Identify the actual decision-makers, such as CEOs or board members, who have the final say.

- *Who's impacted*: Consider those who will feel the effects of the negotiation outcomes, such as employees or community members.

- *Who's influencing behind the scenes*: Recognise the role of influencers who might not be at the table, but whose opinions matter.

- *Who's got a stake in the outcome*: Identify the interested parties who will have an active role or stake in the negotiation, but may not necessarily be at the negotiating table.

- *Who's providing insights*: Value the contributions of subject matter experts and advisers who may be involved and bring specialised knowledge.

- *Who's resolving deadlocks*: Understand the role of mediators or arbitrators in tough negotiation situations and identify who will need to play what role if there is a dispute.

Focus five action list: Who matters in negotiation?

Action	Activity	Done
Map your stakeholders	Create a stakeholder map identifying all the people and groups involved in your negotiation. Include primary counterparts, decision-makers, influencers and impact bearers.	
Understand your counterpart's perspective	Research and understand the needs, motivations and potential Jokers (emotional responses) of your primary counterpart. This will help you anticipate their behaviour and responses.	
Identify influencers	Identify key influencers who can sway the negotiation process. Engage with them to understand their perspectives and build rapport to gain their support.	
Prepare for emotional reactions	Recognise that both you and your counterpart have emotional responses (Jokers) that can affect negotiations. Develop strategies to manage these emotions and stay focused on the negotiation goals.	
Engage experts and advisers	Identify areas where you need specialised knowledge or advice. Engage relevant experts, such as legal advisers or technical consultants, to strengthen your negotiation strategy.	

Chapter 5

When to negotiate

'Now's not the time or place for this conversation.' How many times have you heard someone say that? It's a phrase we've all encountered at one point or another. It's also a powerful reminder of something we often overlook in any conversation, especially in negotiations: timing can be everything.

It's like when we're trying to discuss something important but keep getting interrupted, or we're trying to make a big decision when we're tired—it just doesn't work. That's because timing isn't just about what hour or day it is; it's about when the conditions are right—when people are ready to listen, and when we're ready to make our best case. Just like the old saying goes, 'there's a time and a place for everything'—and that includes negotiating. Negotiation is more than just a set of skills applied when we're 'at the table', it's about knowing when to take action and when to wait.

Sometimes, the best move is to dive right into a discussion. Other times, we need to take a step back, observe and wait for the right moment to speak up or make a move. And, sometimes, the smartest move we can make is to not engage at all. Knowing when to back off and save the discussion for another day can be just as important as knowing when to push forward.

In this chapter, I'm going to guide you through the process of identifying when to negotiate and when not to negotiate so that you recognise the conditions that are most conducive to you getting an agreement.

When the conditions exist

We can't blindly go and start negotiating without first determining if the conditions exist for us to do so. Knowing when to negotiate requires us to consider if:

- there is interest from both sides in negotiating

- there is something of value to exchange

- either party has the authority to negotiate.

If there is no *mutual interest*, it's very difficult to get the other party to the table. Sometimes the interest is obvious; for example, if I want to buy a car and you have one you want to sell. Other times, it's less obvious; for example, if you have a business opportunity for me, but it's not something for which I have expressed a need. In the latter situation, you'd have to create interest for me to consider engaging in a conversation to explore an agreement.

If there is no *mutual value*, it influences the level of interest we have in negotiating. Also, if one party has nothing obvious to gain through the conversation, it's unlikely, they'll come to the table.

If there is no *authority*, it means you or they don't have decision-making authority to either engage in the negotiation itself or to make a call on the final outcome. In a lot of business deals, the person negotiating isn't always the decision-maker, but they do have the authority to negotiate on behalf of the interests of their business and stakeholders.

If there is interest (or opportunity to create interest) and mutual value, and there are people with the authority to negotiate, then we need to look for the signs that the time is right.

When we have signals that the time is right

This signal that the time is right could be a shift in our business environment, such as the unexpected resignation of the CEO, presenting an opportunity for the CFO to negotiate better terms in exchange for maintaining a stable business environment for the board while a successor is recruited. It could be timing a conversation with your landlord about replacing the carpet when you know they are planning to increase the rent at the end of your lease, leveraging the improvement as part of the negotiation. When we know what we want, we can remain alert to the conditions that support the timing of our conversations. It was no surprise that, in the aftermath of the global pandemic, people took the opportunity to negotiate more favourable work-from-home agreements that might not have been possible pre-pandemic. Being aware of the trends and the market conditions enabled many people to have conversations they wouldn't have otherwise had.

When we've assessed the readiness of the other party

We also need to assess the readiness of the other party before we engage them. Asking your line manager to accommodate a change to your working hours at a time when they are feeling overwhelmed with a project may not be the best time. The timing you choose must take into consideration the receptiveness of the other party in reaching a favourable outcome. This doesn't mean avoiding negotiation until there is a perfect time, because there rarely ever is, but creating the appropriate conditions for them to be receptive is key. It could be waiting for the dust to settle after a big company announcement or booking a meeting with your line manager and sending them a summary agenda for their consideration in advance.

When the emotional climate is conducive for agreement

Negotiating in a highly emotionally charged environment isn't easy. Kidnap and crisis negotiators have extensive training over many years to enable them to manage these situations effectively. For the rest of us, it's best that we negotiate in emotionally stable climates wherever possible. It's unlikely we'll get the agreement we want when the environment is pressured. A busy weekend sales environment, where sales assistants are dealing with many customers all at the same time, may not be the best time for you to negotiate the different custom features you want included in your car purchase.

Perhaps a weekday environment when there are fewer people around would be more relaxed for the sales assistant and more conducive to a favourable outcome. Understanding the current environment helps us gauge when to act immediately and when to wait, but another strategic layer involves knowing how to leverage time itself as a negotiating tool.

When being a first mover gives an advantage

In a competitive business scenario, your business may decide to negotiate a merger with a smaller competitor. Approaching them before they are looking to sell or before other competitors notice their potential can give your business an advantage. By negotiating with them before anyone else realises the value available, you may potentially access terms more favourable than during a heated bidding war. Being a first mover in an active negotiation can also give you an advantage by setting initial expectations and creating a starting point, something we'll cover more in Chapter 11.

What I love most is hearing the stories from past clients who have overcome their discomfort and effectively applied the skills they've learned immediately in their business.

Case study: Conflict resolution

Darcy was a general manager for a global technology business selling products into retailers. In one agreement with a retail customer, the terms required DIFOT (delivery in full on time) for a minimum of 98 per cent of orders placed. At the time, Darcy's company was navigating significant supply chain issues and fell short of this key performance indicator.

(continued)

While Darcy and her operations team had been in regular communication with the retailer and had done their very best to secure as much stock as possible, due to global supply chain pressures, they were unable to meet their customer's order fulfilment requirements. Darcy received a communication via email advising that her business would be liable to pay a $390 000 penalty for short supply.

Leveraging the strength of the relationship Darcy had built with her counterpart, she took the proactive step of arranging an in-person meeting and explained that the penalty was unreasonable given global pressures. Her counterpart asked Darcy what she felt was reasonable. Priming her counterpart with mention of the high level of communication and stock management, along with other levels of support that had been provided to the retailer, Darcy positioned herself as a first mover and suggested that her company should not pay anything, and then paused to let her proposal sink in.

After some uncomfortable silence, her counterpart responded by saying her business expected at least $80 000 in reimbursement. This was significant movement and with that Darcy knew she had the opportunity to further reduce the demand. With continued conversations and provision of more supportive discussion points, Darcy was able to gain agreement to a $30 000 penalty instead of the original $390 000.

It was a fantastic financial result, but even more so because she maintained the trust that she had developed in the relationship. She demonstrated to her counterpart that there was more value to be gained through collaboration over the longer term than the immediate benefit of a punitive financial penalty at a time when the supply chain pressures extended globally and were beyond the control of Darcy and her business operations.

In this example, Darcy made sure the emotional climate was conducive to agreement by arranging to meet face to face. If she had responded via email, it would have been unlikely that she would have secured such a sizeable reduction as an email response would have appeared more combative. She also recognised the wider market context and understood that there would only be a short window of time where the global context supported her position that there was disruption in the marketplace. Her opening offer to her counterpart, while uncomfortable, also reframed the discussions, starting the negotiation on price from a much lower benchmark than the initial penalty. By responding swiftly and managing the situation, she was able to avoid escalation of conflict and significantly reduce the financial impact to her business.

When not to negotiate

Understanding when not to negotiate is as crucial as knowing when to initiate the conversation. The importance of gathering and analysing data so you can make informed decisions can't be underestimated. There are times when entering a negotiation may not be the best strategy, and recognising these times can save you from wasting your efforts and being caught in potential conflicts that could have been avoided.

When the other party holds all the leverage

If you don't have any leverage and your position is significantly weaker, entering a negotiation may not be worthwhile. If this is the case, then build your resources and strength first or explore alternative solutions. If the other party has all the leverage, there is no incentive for them to engage unless there is meaningful value to be exchanged. For example, if you are an employee asking for a raise during a period of company-wide budget cuts and redundancies, your position is significantly weaker, and the company has little reason to agree to a salary increase at that time.

When high emotions are involved

In times of high emotional stress, we need to avoid negotiating. Emotions cloud our judgement and can lead to decisions that are not in our best interests. We don't want either of our Jokers at the table trying to make a deal when we know they can be unpredictable under pressure. Trying to negotiate when we're emotionally triggered can escalate into conflict, and our ability to de-escalate a conflict situation is significantly compromised. Also, it's unlikely we'll get the agreement we want when the other party is also emotionally triggered and not in a position to rationally assess the value in the deal we're seeking to make. In scenarios such as divorce agreements and custody agreements, we need to approach settlement negotiations when everyone is composed and calm, potentially with the help of a mediator.

When you're lacking preparation

I've observed too many negotiations go south due to lack of preparation, whether it's because critical information was missed, the other party's interests weren't discovered, stakeholders weren't aligned or the goal wasn't clearly identified. If you're unprepared, postpone the negotiation until you are ready and have all the relevant information to have a robust conversation and be able to make an informed decision. Don't be rushed into conversations you're not ready for, as we know it's as important to manage our state as it is for us to manage the other party's. In this context, 'state' refers to your mental and emotional condition. Being calm, focused and confident can significantly impact the negotiation process and outcomes, while being stressed, anxious or distracted can impact your ability to effectively communicate and make sound decisions.

When ethical concerns arise

It's not beyond the realm of possibility that you may receive incentives from a counterparty to encourage your agreement to a deal; for example, a supplier might offer you personal gifts or financial kickbacks to secure a contract. Alternatively, you may be in a position of power where a counterpart might seek to draw you into a conflict situation, such as provoking you to make a decision that could be seen as favouritism or unfair treatment. This could be used against you later, where any perceived abuse of power would be open to investigation. Be aware of anything that might compromise your ethical and moral standards and potentially involve you in legal issues. In any situation where you feel that there is a potential for ethical concerns, reject negotiations outright and report any unethical behaviour to the appropriate regulatory bodies.

When the relationship costs outweigh the benefits

Sometimes pushing too hard can damage relationships with key stakeholders or partners, so we have to assess whether the outcome of the negotiation is worth the potential relationship strain. This is particularly important in scenarios where long-term collaboration is more valuable than a single agreement. For example, you might negotiate a highly favourable revenue split for a single event collaboration with another business; while you gain more revenue from this one deal, the partner feels the split is unfair and is hesitant to collaborate on future, potentially more lucrative, events. You might have secured more favourable terms in the short term, but you have potentially lost a valuable partnership that could be significantly more valuable to you in the long term.

When you have a better alternative

If you already have a better option that far exceeds the value that this negotiation would bring, then it's most likely not worth your time engaging. Options give us power, so identify your options before determining if it's worth your time, energy and resources negotiating.

When you stand to lose more than you gain

In certain situations, the cost of negotiating is more than you stand to gain through engaging. It can often become a point of contention for our ego, the Joker, who may feel it's not right or unjust in some way that the other party can walk away with a perceived 'win' and no consequences in certain situations. The key here is to objectively and rationally evaluate if it's worth the resources to negotiate. Typically, it's not when the available upside on agreement is much less than the cost incurred to get it. For example, you might have a disagreement with your partner over which movie to watch and, instead of letting the debate escalate, you choose to let your partner pick a movie, even if it's not something you want to watch, because the fleeting satisfaction of asserting your preference isn't worth the loss of a peaceful evening together.

When the outcome is of little importance

You don't have to engage in a negotiation where the outcome is of little importance. Why bother at all if the outcomes of agreement or the consequences of no agreement are of little concern? Choosing where we place our time and energy is important. If we know what we value, then it can be easier to avoid our focus being directed on situations of little importance.

Case study: Mel and Ed's business partnership follow-up

When Mel dissolved the partnership with Ed back on page 61, she chose not to pursue him for the repayment of the director salary costs that had been paid out of her business. Even though she was entitled to be repaid, she chose not to expend any further energy dealing with Ed and his businesses. She took the financial hit knowing that she'd recover her losses faster by giving her full energy to growing her business than letting her focus be distracted by further legal action and her business incurring further costs in legal fees to recover the money. She took an objective and pragmatic approach, and while her inner Joker would have quite happily pushed for her to take Ed to task over his unscrupulous actions, thankfully, Mel engaged her ACE and decided to move on with her life.

(continued)

Within a few short weeks she'd rebranded her business and, with renewed excitement and confidence in herself, won several new clients. This demonstrated that focusing on what she valued and doing work she loved with clients she adored was going to be far more rewarding than engaging in a fight with someone who'd already demonstrated that their moral compass wasn't working.

When to wait

Patience is a virtue, especially in negotiation. Sometimes, the best move we can make is not to move at all, at least, not yet. Waiting can be a powerful strategy, giving us time to gather information, understand the other party better and even allow them to reveal more about their position.

Patience doesn't mean inaction.

Patience is about waiting for the right moment to act. Sometimes this means carefully observing changes in the other person's behaviour, such as picking up a shift in their tone or body language. Spotting these subtle cues can inform us when the right time is to move forward.

I regularly observe corporate leaders interrupting their counterpart before they have finished making their proposal, often missing the opportunity to find out exactly what was being offered. If only they would patiently listen and not immediately counter every point, they'd gather invaluable insights into the other party's priorities and eventually negotiate a deal that was beneficial for both sides.

When there is resistance or tension

We can do more harm than good if we try to move forward when the other party isn't willing or able. If you sense tension or resistance, recognise that pushing too hard might lead to a breakdown in communication, or worse, deadlock. Sometimes, by stepping back and giving the situation some space to breathe, you give it a better chance of a successful outcome. The key is to use patience effectively by balancing it with timely action. Waiting too long can be perceived as indecisiveness or a lack of interest. Real strength lies in knowing when to pause and when to proceed, which comes from experience, intuition and careful observation.

When the situation is sensitive

Negotiating with family or friends can be especially delicate. Unlike business negotiations, these discussions involve deep emotional stakes that can significantly affect your relationships. It's not just about finding the most convenient time or making a logical argument; it's about choosing the right moment with care and consideration for the feelings involved.

When to leverage time

In negotiation, time is a powerful lever that can be skilfully used to give you an advantage. Time pressures and deadlines are common in negotiation, so understanding how to navigate them and avoid being adversely affected by them is key.

When it comes to time, it's helpful to remember that it's usually the party without the pressure of time on their side that will be at an advantage, as they have the opportunity to explore options and aren't driven by deadlines. For example, a buyer looking for a new home to purchase when they don't have one to sell has more opportunity to find the perfect place and explore more options than the buyer who is up against a tight deadline.

When we need to create urgency

Deadlines create a sense of urgency that push us to make decisions quickly. It's common to see us make deals and decisions quicker under time pressure than we would without the pressure. The deals we are willing to accept can also be less attractive than the ones we would accept if time was abundant. If you're seeking commitment from the other party, putting a deadline on your proposal is a helpful way to keep the conversation progressing at a reasonable pace. Be aware of the approach you're taking: in a competitive negotiation, increasing time pressure can put the other party on the back foot, which can increase the advantage you have; in a collaborative negotiation, you want to give adequate time for consideration while still ensuring conversations are progressing.

When we need to focus discussions

Setting a time limit for negotiations can help keep discussions focused and productive. It prevents the process from dragging on and can motivate both parties to prioritise their most important points. Sometimes, extending the deadline before negotiating can be the best move to give you an opportunity to gather more data, build relationships or give time for the external market conditions to move in your favour.

When timing has a direct impact on our specific goal

Our timing in negotiation needs to align with what we're trying to achieve. It's like setting up a series of dominos; when we tap the first one at the right time, everything else falls into place as planned. Understanding what we're trying to achieve is a prerequisite to determining the most optimal timing. If you have short-term goals that require a quick resolution, then you may need to be more aggressive with your timeline and more tactical with the use of time.

If your goals are more long-term focused, such as building a long-term partnership, then expecting to finalise a deal in a few short weeks may not be appropriate, given that depth of connection and trust can take time to develop. It may be more appropriate to space out the negotiation, allowing time to thoroughly evaluate the terms, build trust and develop the relationship on a solid foundation. Our end goals and what we value significantly influence when and how we negotiate and, ultimately, how successful we are in getting the outcomes we want.

Case study: Procurement negotiation

In one negotiation, my client, a procurement manager of a large technology retailer, was exploring the purchase of CCTV cameras for all their retail stores. While the store upgrades were required over the coming 12 months, there wasn't any immediate urgency to procure cameras until they found an acceptable deal. Through their interactions and discussions with one prospective international supplier, they noticed that all the proposals from them were based on the deal being closed before the end of April.

(continued)

Upon further exploration and information gathering, they determined that it was the company's quarter end and the subtle sense of urgency they had picked up from the account manager's tone suggested there were targets they may have needed to hit. Not certain that their hypothesis was the correct one, they strategically tested their assumptions by sharing with the prospective supplier that they weren't in any immediate rush, which was true, and as such, would continue to explore options and would return to him in May.

By taking their time, they demonstrated their confidence and control of the situation and that they valued making the right decision, not a hasty one. This strategic use of time as a lever increased the pressure on the supplier's account manager because the timing of the deal was incredibly valuable to him, even though he had not divulged this openly. Their patience and alignment of their internal team to wait without any further action to be taken paid off — the supplier came back with an improved offer the following week, a deal with much more favourable terms offered on the condition that the agreement could be signed before the end of April. The parties agreed to a deal, which saved the business over $600 000 in costs.

It was a powerful example of time being appropriately and ethically used as a strategic lever for a positive outcome. Remember, while time can be a powerful negotiating tool, be cautious not to let others manipulate this advantage against you.

Time to check in with yourself

Reflecting on past negotiations is a valuable practice for honing your timing skills. In a recent negotiation, personally or professionally:

- When did the negotiations take place?

- How did timing influence the outcome?

- Did you rush the negotiations?

- Did you wait too long to address critical issues?

- Was the other party in the right frame of mind for negotiations to be effective?

By analysing what happened, you can learn a great deal about the impact of timing on negotiation outcomes. For example, you might realise that a negotiation that you conducted under time pressure led to concessions that could have been avoided with more careful planning and patience. Keeping a journal of your reflections can be particularly useful, allowing you to track patterns in your negotiation approach and improve over time—after all, we can't change what we can't see.

Now that we've considered when we'll negotiate, next we'll look at where to negotiate and what you need to consider with the different place options you have available.

Negotiation nuggets:
When to negotiate

- *When checking conditions*: Always determine if the timing is right before you start negotiating. Make sure there is mutual interest, something valuable to exchange and that all parties have the authority to make decisions.

- *When considering timing*: Recognise that the right moment can vastly improve your negotiation outcome. Whether it's capitalising on an opportunity or choosing a calm time to discuss the matter, timing can significantly influence the deal.

- *When thinking about not negotiating*: If you're in a weak position, unprepared or the costs outweigh the benefits, it might be better to wait for a more favourable time.

- *When using time as a tool*: Create urgency to hasten decisions when it benefits you, but also know when to slow things down and use patience to your advantage.

- *When aligning strategies with goals*: Consider whether you need a fast solution or a steady, enduring relationship. Your approach should reflect your ultimate objectives.

- *When managing emotions*: Aim to negotiate in stable, calm environments. High emotions can complicate discussions and lead to poor decisions.

Focus five action list: When to negotiate?

Action	Activity	Done
Evaluate readiness	Before engaging, assess if both parties are ready and willing to negotiate. Ensure there is mutual interest, value to exchange and authority to make decisions.	
Assess timing and environment	Choose the right time and place. Avoid high-stress or emotionally charged environments and aim for a setting where both parties can focus and communicate effectively.	
Use timing as a lever	Leverage timing strategically. Recognise when being a first mover or creating a sense of urgency can give you an advantage. Avoid rushing into negotiations without preparation.	
Identify when not to negotiate	Recognise situations where negotiating may not be beneficial, such as when the other party holds all the leverage, emotions are high or you are unprepared. Postpone negotiations if necessary.	
Reflect on timing	After each negotiation, reflect on how timing influenced the outcome. Determine whether the negotiation was rushed or if critical issues were addressed at the right time. Use these reflections to improve future negotiations.	

Chapter 6

Where to negotiate

As we move on from considering the appropriate timing of negotiations, it's equally important to focus on the place where these conversations occur. The setting we choose does more than just frame what we say, it plays a crucial role in how smoothly we can navigate towards an agreement.

Sometimes the timing is right, but if the place isn't, it creates a significant imbalance in the negotiation dynamics. Timing and place are both crucial elements that contribute to the success of a negotiation, and they often have a symbiotic relationship.

Imagine a situation where you and your partner have been planning to have a serious discussion about financial planning, budgeting and possibly making some significant investments. You've both been waiting for the right time when you're not stressed from work and can devote your full attention to this important topic. Finally, a relaxing

Sunday afternoon presents itself. The timing seems perfect—it's a quiet day, no work-related pressures and you both are in the right mindset to discuss finances.

However, the place you end up having this discussion is not ideal: it's at your dining table while your kids are playing loudly in the living room. You thought it would be fine since it's a familiar and comfortable spot in your home, but the constant noise and interruptions from your children make it difficult to focus and have a meaningful conversation.

It's a simple example, but often, the significance of a negotiation's setting is underestimated. Whether it's the comfort of our own office or the increasingly familiar virtual meeting spaces, each environment influences not just the negotiation process, but also how readily agreements are reached. Therefore, our strategy should be tailored to align with the chosen location, whether the negotiation is synchronous or asynchronous.

Think about this: Is the location I'm choosing for this conversation facilitating a smoother path to agreement?

Selecting your negotiation venue is about more than convenience or logistics; it's about creating an environment conducive to agreement. The choice of location sets the tone of the negotiation and can sway the negotiation style, influencing whether interactions are real-time or asynchronous, face to face or virtual. These decisions don't just affect the atmosphere for all parties involved, they also subtly hint at the balance of power dynamics. The locations we select are instrumental in not only shaping the discussion, but also in how readily and effectively an agreement can be reached.

What has sport got to do with where we negotiate?

Despite my casual interest in Formula 1 racing, I'm not what you'd call a sports enthusiast. However, when it comes to illustrating the importance of place in negotiations, I find sports analogies particularly effective and relatable. In sports, the concepts of home ground and away ground are fundamental. Teams playing on their home ground often enjoy a certain edge, supported by familiar surroundings and cheering fans. In contrast, the away games come with their set of challenges: unfamiliar territory and a lack of home support.

This analogy from the sports world beautifully mirrors the dynamics of business negotiations. Being on your home ground, where you feel most comfortable, can give you a strategic advantage in negotiations. Conversely, when negotiating in an away setting, dominated by the other party, you need a different set of tactics and adaptability.

In understanding this sports-inspired concept of place, we can more effectively create the negotiation strategies that move us towards gaining agreement. I'll take you through the common places you have available and what you need to be aware of with each.

Negotiating on your home ground

In your own space, you have the upper hand because of familiarity. This familiar setting, your home ground, is where you're at your best, surrounded by what you know and what's comfortable. This isn't just about physical comfort, it's about psychological readiness. You know the layout, you have easy access to your resources and you control the environment. This level of comfort and control can translate into you taking a more confident approach in negotiations.

To bring this to life, here are two different examples where home ground makes a difference:

Job interviews held at your current workplace

Imagine you're being considered for a promotion within your current company, and the interview is held in your own office or a familiar conference room. This setting, where you've already established your presence and reputation, can give you a distinct advantage. You're more at ease in familiar surroundings, can showcase your achievements in a real-life context and likely feel more confident responding to questions in a known environment. This home ground familiarity can positively impact your performance in the interview.

Sales pitches at your company headquarters

When hosting potential clients for a sales pitch at your company headquarters, there's a home ground advantage. You can control the presentation environment, use your technology and resources seamlessly, and even give a tour showcasing your company's operations and culture. This familiarity and control can make your pitch more persuasive and tailored, leaving a lasting impression on the client.

Case study: As Jack Reacher would say, 'details matter'

Having worked in the UK's fast-moving consumer goods industry for many years, it wasn't uncommon to invite customers to our head office to visit manufacturing facilities. Whenever we expected customers onsite, there was a protocol to follow. Everything regarding the customer visit would be meticulously planned, from the moment they arrived and who would greet them, to the route they would take to the meeting room and what they would see along the way. This included what the customers would see on internal whiteboards, in open-plan office areas and on walls en route to the bathrooms.

It even extended to what conversations were to be had in corridors, who they would encounter and who they wouldn't. The entire head office would know when a customer was onsite. It was a great opportunity to learn and understand the level of detail that was being considered. These contracts were worth millions of pounds annually, so there was no complacency. While the home ground presents an opportunity for an advantage, it's important not to underestimate the level of preparation that goes into maximising it.

Home ground: SWOT

In the SWOT analysis in table 6.1, I've highlighted the various internal and external factors that influence the outcome of negotiations conducted on your home ground, with insights into how to leverage strengths and opportunities while addressing weaknesses and threats.

Table 6.1 the factors that influence home ground negotiations

Strengths	Weaknesses
Familiarity and comfort Control over environment Resource accessibility Psychological advantage	Overconfidence Perceived intimidation Echo chamber risk
Opportunities	**Threats**
Showcase company culture and values Strengthen relationships Leverage technological advantages	Complacency in preparation Negative power perception Unexpected disruptions

Strategies for maximising your home ground advantage in negotiations

- *Balancing power dynamics:* While leveraging your home ground advantage, be mindful of how the other party perceives this setting. If you're seeking to create value through the negotiation, create an environment that is welcoming and inclusive, not intimidating. This approach helps establish a foundation for open, collaborative dialogue. You can do this by arranging seating in a non-confrontational set-up, offering refreshments and actively encouraging input from the other party.

- *Thorough preparation:* Don't fall into the trap of complacency just because you're in a familiar setting. Prepare for the negotiation as diligently as you would if you were stepping into the other party's territory. This includes researching the other party's background, understanding their objectives and potential negotiation tactics, and being prepared to address their concerns. Additionally, have a clear agenda and a well-thought-out strategy to guide the discussion.

- *Wise use of resources:* Your home ground provides easy access to various resources, but it's crucial to use them strategically. This could mean having key team members available for quick consultations, using technology to effectively present data or proposals, and ensuring all necessary materials are at hand without overwhelming the space. The goal is to enhance the negotiation experience, demonstrating professionalism and preparedness, without making the other party feel inundated or disadvantaged.

- *Creating a conducive atmosphere:* The physical setting plays a significant role in the negotiation's tone. Ensure the meeting space is comfortable, well-lit and free from interruptions. Consider aspects like temperature, lighting and noise levels. By creating a well-arranged environment, you can subconsciously ease tensions and promote a more productive discussion.

- *Engage in listening to understand:* Use your familiarity with the environment to focus more on listening to understand. Being in a comfortable space can allow you to concentrate better on what the other party is saying, leading to more effective responses and a deeper understanding of their perspective.

Negotiating on your home ground offers many advantages, but it also requires careful handling of power dynamics and preparation. We've all heard stories about gameplay in sports, like turning down the temperature in the changing room for the away team or soaking it in water to make the environment uncomfortable for them. Tactics and games like these set the tone for the relationship and will influence the behaviour you receive in response. In business and personal negotiations, be aware of the aspects I've mentioned and use your home ground setting strategically. Create an environment that is conducive to achieving a mutual agreement while maintaining a positive relationship with the other party.

Negotiating on the other party's home ground

When negotiating on the other party's home ground, it would be natural to feel a bit apprehensive, but it's important to remember that the opportunity for a successful outcome is still very much available.

The location you choose is there to facilitate a smoother path to agreement. The key focus when you are on away ground is that you need to be adaptable, observant and think ahead in your strategy. This is not too dissimilar from your home ground, but it's important to acknowledge that the environment presents greater uncertainty.

Over my career and in my personal life I've negotiated on the away ground on many occasions, whether it be the home ground of retail giants both in the UK and in Australia, multinational suppliers or that of the executive board when seeking agreement on investment proposals. I've always found these settings to be of great value. It's easy to accept the default that home ground always has the advantage, but your skill set and acumen is only really tested in unfamiliar territory and in putting yourself out of your comfort zone. When smoothing the path to agreement, the focus needs to be on building depth within relationships and showing humility. The outcomes are more important than the false sense of significance being on home ground gives you.

To bring this to life here are two examples where 'away ground' makes a difference.

International business expansion

Imagine your company is seeking to expand its operations into a new international market. You are part of the leadership team that travels to the target country to negotiate with potential local partners. Negotiating on this away ground gives you invaluable insights into the local business culture, market dynamics and consumer behaviour. Being there in person allows you to observe subtleties that aren't apparent in remote communications, enabling you to tailor your approach to align with local expectations and norms. This direct engagement can significantly impact the success of your expansion strategy.

Vendor and supplier agreement

You're a retail buyer visiting a manufacturer's facility to negotiate a new supply contract. By conducting negotiations at the manufacturer's site, you gain a better understanding of the production capacity, quality control processes and work environment. This direct observation can influence the negotiation terms regarding quality standards, delivery schedules and pricing. The face-to-face interaction helps in building a stronger, more transparent relationship with your supplier, which is beneficial for long-term business collaboration.

Away ground: SWOT

As with the home ground, in the SWOT in table 6.2, I've highlighted the various internal and external factors that influence the outcome of negotiations conducted on away ground, with insights into how to leverage strengths and opportunities while addressing weaknesses and threats.

Table 6.2 the factors that influence away ground negotiations

Strengths	Weaknesses
Expanding your perspective of the other party Enhancing resilience and adaptability In-depth cultural insight Demonstrating collaboration	Unfamiliarity with the environment Limited control over logistics Dependency on external resources Potential for being underestimated
Opportunities	**Threats**
Fostering stronger business relationships Networking and connection building Demonstrating your versatility Learning and skill enhancement	Power imbalance dynamics Unforeseen situational challenges Managing stress in new settings Navigating cultural differences

To minimise the disadvantage of negotiating on away ground, consider these specific strategies

- *In-depth research and understanding:* Go beyond just preparing for the negotiation subject. Deeply research the other party's background, market position and cultural nuances. This understanding will help you anticipate their strategies and align your approach accordingly.

- *Cultural sensitivity and adaptability:* Be particularly sensitive to cultural nuances, especially in international settings. Adaptability is key; be ready to adjust your communication style, body language and negotiation tactics to suit the setting and the other party's expectations.

- *Strategic positioning and seating arrangements:* In away ground scenarios, even the seating arrangement can impact the negotiation. If possible, suggest a seating layout that feels collaborative rather than confrontational. Positioning yourself strategically in the room, for example, sitting where you can see everyone clearly or in close proximity to the decision-makers, can also help in maintaining confidence and control.

- *Mental preparation for power dynamics:* Prepare mentally for the dynamics of negotiating in the other party's space. Anticipate scenarios where you might feel at a disadvantage and strategise on how to stay composed and assertive.

- *Building rapport and finding common ground:* Establishing rapport is crucial. Look for common interests or shared connections as a foundation for building trust. Use empathy and active listening to create a connection, making the other party more open to collaboration.

- *Neutral venue as a backup:* If you sense overwhelming power imbalances, have a suggestion for a neutral venue ready as a backup. Shifting to neutral ground, even for a portion of the negotiation, can help in rebalancing the dynamics.

- *Effective use of breaks and timeouts:* In an away ground setting, don't hesitate to use breaks or timeouts strategically. Use this time to regroup, reassess your strategy or consult with your team if needed.

- *Post-negotiation reflection:* After the negotiation, take time to reflect on the experience. Analyse the impact of the away ground on the negotiation process and outcome. Use these insights to better prepare for future negotiations in similar settings.

Negotiating on away ground will always present a unique set of challenges and opportunities. It demands a blend of thorough preparation, adaptability and psychological readiness. If you embrace these elements, you can turn a seemingly daunting situation into a constructive and potentially advantageous negotiation experience.

Negotiating on neutral ground

Choosing neutral ground for negotiations can be a strategic move, particularly in high-stakes or sensitive discussions. It's about finding a place that isn't tied to either party, creating an environment of impartiality. My first encounter with the concept of neutral ground was as a child in family court during my parents' custody negotiations. This setting was all about creating a fair, balanced space for making important decisions.

In business, the rationale behind selecting a neutral location is to strip away any home ground advantage, levelling the playing field for all involved. Whether it's a third-party office, a public venue or a digital platform, neutral ground serves as a stage where negotiations can unfold without the usual power dynamics. This can lead to more open, honest conversations, as the usual territorial influences are absent. It's an opportunity for both parties to focus purely on the negotiation itself, undistracted by their usual environments.

However, negotiating on neutral ground doesn't come without its challenges. There's a lack of control over the environment, which can mean facing logistical issues or unfamiliar technology setups. Being in a space that's new to both parties requires a degree of adaptability and attention to detail that might not be necessary in more familiar settings.

On the flip side, the potential for building mutual respect is significant. When you meet someone halfway, in a literal sense, it signals a readiness to find common solutions and work collaboratively. I've seen examples of this with large retail buyers meeting smaller suppliers in coffee shops to demonstrate willingness to work together. Such settings often foster creativity, as being outside of the usual work environment can inspire fresh perspectives and new approaches to problem-solving.

But it's important to remember that neutral doesn't always mean ideal. Unexpected challenges such as background noise or inadequate facilities can arise. Preparing for these eventualities is key. Scouting the venue in advance and being ready to tweak your communication style to suit the atmosphere can help navigate these issues.

Mastering negotiations in neutral settings is about embracing the equity and openness of these environments, while also being alert to their unique challenges. It involves thorough preparation, the ability to adapt and a commitment to finding common ground. This approach can turn a neutral space into a productive setting for resolution and agreement. In essence, success in these situations hinges on your readiness to adapt, your attention to detail and your willingness to engage openly and with care.

Negotiating virtually

The COVID-19 pandemic not only accelerated our use of virtual negotiation platforms, but also fundamentally changed our approach to negotiations. This paradigm shift is no longer a matter of necessity or convenience, but a change in how we interact, understand and influence others in the negotiation process.

Traditionally, 'place' in negotiations meant a physical location, a setting where parties would meet face to face. Today's negotiation landscape is more fluid, incorporating both the physical and the virtual. While tools like video conferencing, emails, phone calls and instant messaging have long been part of a negotiator's toolkit, their use has become more prevalent and integral to the process. Now, some of these tools are not just supplementary options, but the primary channels for negotiation.

The good news is the virtual negotiation environment brings several strengths: the convenience and accessibility of being able to negotiate from anywhere; saving valuable time without the need for travel; it's also more cost-effective, without many of the expenses associated with traditional, in-person negotiations. Additionally, our ability to record meetings on these platforms can provide a clear record of discussions, a crucial aspect in maintaining transparency and accountability.

There is also a significant downside to our reliance on technology in negotiations. It limits our ability to read body language, which can lead to us missing key information needed to validate what is being communicated verbally. This is a significant disadvantage considering the role non-verbal cues play in traditional negotiation settings. The high potential for distractions in our personal environments also impacts the level of focus and engagement we can give. Not to mention how common issues such as our tech set-up, the differences in the digital platform each party prefers using and connectivity challenges can, and do, disrupt the flow of discussions.

We also can't and typically won't know who else is in the 'room' on a virtual negotiation, so discussing sensitive information could be a challenge and a high level of trust is required for us to do so. Our ability to create the appropriate conditions for the other party and our joint discussion are also limited to what we control in our virtual environment, not theirs.

Despite these challenges, virtual negotiations do offer remarkable opportunities. The reach is now global, allowing us to connect with potential partners across the world without the traditional geographical limitations. The flexibility in scheduling afforded by digital platforms is unmatched; we can accommodate different time zones and schedules with relative ease. The use of digital tools also enhances our ability to share information and data instantly, making negotiations more dynamic and interactive too.

Yet, we do have to acknowledge that, as technology becomes more sophisticated, so do the threats—and navigating cybersecurity risks is a key consideration that organisations will need to directly address.

Preparing thoroughly for these virtual negotiations means making sure we're:

- comfortable

- proficient with the technology

- focusing on clear, concise communication

- in a distraction-free environment

- building trust through rapport virtually

- diligently following up with clear documentation.

A word on artificial intelligence

For large organisations, sophisticated artificial intelligence is already being used in negotiations, both as a source of negotiation intelligence and as expertise for optimising the process as well as maximising the deal value. This integration signifies a crucial shift, not just in how we negotiate, because more commercial negotiations will happen autonomously, but also in how the dynamics of human intelligence and artificial intelligence will be balanced in the future of negotiation.

While there is a lot changing with technology advancing in this space, we'll need to blend traditional in-person negotiation acumen with a mastery of digital tools and platforms. Sophisticated technology is often undermined when the people using it don't have the skills to leverage it.

Negotiating on email

Email conversations are the fastest route to being misunderstood. While email as a tool is great for communicating facts and documenting agreements, it's certainly not the tool you should be using for negotiating. Yet, while I don't recommend email as a tool for negotiating, it's important to acknowledge that I do often see it being used for this purpose. Email stands out for its ubiquity and convenience, especially if you're communicating across time zones. However, communicating this way tends to encourage more competitive behaviour and it's necessary to understand the risks associated with it. If social media trolling behaviour is any example of how people get 'brave' when they're behind a keyboard, then email negotiating in a professional environment has the propensity for people to be more aggressive in their demands and say things they wouldn't dare say in person.

We've all, no doubt, experienced more than one situation in which we've sent an email, and the response has suggested that other party has entirely misunderstood what we were communicating. I've seen countless examples in my corporate career where people, me included, have gone down the rabbit hole of responding, in reaction to what was received, and before you know it, have a thread of back-and-forth emails moving each party further and further away from consensus and agreement.

The written nature of email leaves room for misinterpretation of tone and intent, both of which are attributed by the receiving party and are influenced by their own emotions and situation at the time. The signal we have sent, whether intentional or not, isn't always received in the same way we've intended. A statement meant to be neutral can be perceived as confrontational, potentially escalating a situation that was intended to be collaborative into a competitive scenario. The absence of non-verbal cues and real-time feedback creates a disconnect, making each party more prone to adopting rigid or aggressive positions.

The asynchronous nature of email allows each party more time to analyse and strategise, often leading to more calculated, competitive responses rather than spontaneous, collaborative solutions. How many times have you spun round in your chair and asked a colleague to read an email you've received and ascertain if they interpret the meaning of the email the same way you have? Before you know it, there are four people reading the email over your shoulder, each adding their perspective on what it means. Emails lack personal interaction so it's natural for them to lead to a more competitive and less collaborative negotiation atmosphere. Building trust and rapport is essential in negotiations, and the impersonal nature of email hinders this process.

When it comes to negotiations, email is best used for sharing facts, scheduling meetings or confirming agreed-upon points, rather than actual negotiating. If you must use email for any other reason, be clear and precise in language, and avoid emotional content that can be easily misinterpreted. Be very aware that misunderstandings are common, and the depth of conversation necessary for complex negotiations will not be achieved on email. If you have any sense that discussions are becoming more complex and potentially contentious, you must transition to a more interactive communication method, such as a phone call or a face-to-face meeting where you can have real-time discussions, allowing for immediate clarification and a more personal connection than email.

Negotiating by phone

In a world where instant messaging and emails are the norm, the significance of a phone call in negotiations can't be overstated. Despite our growing reliance on digital communication, there's something about a phone conversation that can change the entire course of a negotiation. The immediacy and personal connection that comes with a phone call can often bridge the gap left by emails or instant messages. Especially in scenarios that need quick decisions, such as a real estate agent negotiating a deal, the ability to communicate directly, respond promptly and convey sincerity through voice can be game changing.

However, phone negotiations come with their unique set of challenges. When you can't see the person you are talking to, understanding their intentions and feelings becomes more about listening to their tone and choice of words. It's crucial to pay attention to these subtleties. Also, phone calls can sometimes catch you off guard, and it's essential to know how to handle such situations. If you find yourself unexpectedly on a call that requires negotiation, a good practise is to take a moment to gather your thoughts. Don't hesitate to ask for a brief pause if needed, or even suggest rescheduling the call if it means you'll be better prepared.

To navigate phone negotiations effectively, preparation is key. Know what you want to achieve from the conversation and have any necessary information ready. A quiet environment can help you focus better and ensure clarity in communication. It's equally important to be a good listener, tuning into the nuances of the other person's voice to gauge their stance and emotions.

Remember, the way you use your voice can greatly influence the negotiation. Adjusting your tone, pacing, and even the volume can help convey your message more effectively.

Imagine you're negotiating a contract extension with a key client over the phone, and they are expressing concerns about the cost. By using a warm and empathetic tone, you can convey your understanding and build rapport. By slowing your pace of speech, you help de-escalate their stress and allow for a more thoughtful conversation. In lowering your volume, you help calm their frustrations and create a more collaborative atmosphere where they feel heard and respected, making them more open to finding a mutually beneficial solution.

Mastering phone negotiations is about combining preparation, effective communication and active listening. It's an invaluable skill in today's business world, where being able to negotiate well over the phone can set you apart. Even in an age dominated by emails and instant messaging, the power of a well-handled phone call in negotiations remains undiminished.

Negotiation nuggets:
Where to negotiate

- *When considering the location*: Always think critically about the setting where the negotiation will take place. The environment can significantly influence the dynamics and outcome of your discussions.

- *When choosing a familiar venue*: Use your home ground advantage when appropriate. Negotiating in a place where you feel comfortable and in control can enhance your confidence and authority during discussions.

- *When stepping into their space*: Be prepared and adaptable when negotiating in unfamiliar settings (the away ground). Understanding and respecting the other party's home advantage can help you tailor your strategies effectively.

- *When opting for neutral ground*: Consider neutral venues to eliminate power imbalances that could affect the negotiation. Neutral settings can foster a more equitable and focused negotiation environment.

- *When negotiating virtually*: Embrace the challenges and opportunities of virtual negotiations. Ensure you are familiar with the technology and create a professional, distraction-free environment to maintain focus and effectiveness.

- *When communication is digital (email)*: Recognise that email negotiations can easily lead to misunderstandings due to the lack of non-verbal cues. Use emails for confirming details and follow-ups, not for conducting the entire negotiation.

- *When discussing over the phone*: Use phone calls for negotiations that require a personal touch without the logistical need for face-to-face meetings. Be mindful of your tone and clarity since visual cues are absent.

- *When the setting could impact negotiation dynamics*: Be strategic about the location you use. The right environment can provide psychological comfort and power, and a more successful negotiation outcome.

Focus five action list: Where to negotiate?

Action	Activity	Done
Choose the right setting	Select the best location for negotiation: home ground for control and comfort; away ground for understanding the other party; or neutral ground for balanced power dynamics. Tailor your approach to each setting.	
Prepare for the environment	Collect relevant documents, study the other party's background and predict possible obstacles. Develop a detailed agenda and a strategic plan to use your strengths and address potential weaknesses.	
Adapt to virtual negotiations	Agree on a digital platform that both parties are comfortable with. Ensure you have the necessary technical skills, establish clear communication protocols and eliminate distractions for focused discussions.	
Avoid negotiating by email	Use email for sharing facts, scheduling meetings or confirming points. For complex negotiations, transition to phone calls or face-to-face meetings to ensure clarity and rapport.	
Leverage phone negotiations	Use phone calls for direct, immediate communication. Focus on tone, pacing and volume to convey empathy and build rapport. Always follow up with a summary email to document the agreement.	

Part II
The 'how' of negotiating with the Value Method

After laying the groundwork with the foundations, you're ready to move into *how* to negotiate using the keys provided in the Value Method. Here's a summary of the five keys to achieving value and what we'll cover in each chapter.

Key 1: Identify the Value

You're addressing two critical questions What do you value? and What do they value? This process requires time to reflect on both your own interests and needs, as well as those of the other party. When identifying what they value, you're not simply asking *what* they want; you're seeking to understand the *why* behind it—your objective is to get to the heart of what they truly value. This understanding will help you more effectively identify the value you have to exchange in return and whether there is an opportunity for more value to be created and grown through your agreement together.

Key 2: Analyse the data

Here you are gathering and analysing data, transforming it into information that you can harness as a source of power and confidence. Here you'll apply three different perspectives—yours, theirs and an objective viewpoint—to the data you have collected to help you:

- better understand the people you're negotiating with

- prepare your proposals with confidence

- anticipate the other party's counter perspectives.

With the data you'll analyse, you will clearly identify your goals for the negotiation, your walk-away position, the variables and levers available for negotiation, the concessions you're willing to make and your next best options if the deal doesn't materialise. Additionally, you will have considered the other party's likely position.

Key 3: Understand your Leverage

Navigating a negotiation requires an understanding of the leverage and power you possess to influence the other party towards an agreement. We'll explore how leverage can be actual or perceived and how you can effectively influence the perception of your power and protect yourself from others who default to using force. We'll also discuss how you can optimise outcomes and maintain relationships by using power, and the appropriate influencing principles, ethically. We'll also discuss the notion of fairness and why it doesn't always lead to the most optimal outcomes for all parties involved.

Key 4: Embrace feeling Uncomfortable

Embarking on a negotiation means stepping outside of our comfort zone and getting comfortable with feeling uncomfortable. This is where we explore your triggers and how you actively manage your emotions through both verbal and non-verbal communication so that you avoid leaking value. We'll look at how to focus on the other party and identify what might be going on in their heads and limit how often your emotional Joker takes up residence at the negotiation table.

Key 5: Execute the plan

As much as the theory is useful, we only get better when we put it into practise. Here we'll look at how you should set the scene, prime and position your value as well as align internal stakeholders. Then when you're ready for the negotiation, we'll cover how to negotiate and reach your desired agreement. Negotiation doesn't just end 'at the table' so we'll wrap up with what you need to do afterwards too.

As you read on, keep in mind that the depth of your planning should match the complexity of your negotiation; however, the core components we discuss will be applicable to any negotiation you undertake.

Chapter 7

V — Identify your value

Former American boxer, Bernard Hopkins, once said, 'If you don't know your own value, somebody will tell you your value, and it will be less than you're worth'. I've learned that, whether you're negotiating at an individual level or on behalf of your business, one thing is certain: if you fail to recognise your value, or the value that your business brings to the table, then you leave yourself exposed to having your value defined by the other party. And if you're in a negotiation, it's more than likely to be less than what you're worth.

Of course, it doesn't need to be this way. That's why I believe that you should deepen your knowledge of how value is determined for yourself, your business and for others. When you understand value, it's your first key to maximising it.

Understanding the need to feel valued

Before you can understand value and how it's determined, I need you to acknowledge and accept the significant role our human psychology plays when it comes to negotiation. As complex human beings, our approach to negotiation is inherently emotional, not just logical. Understanding this emotional dimension is essential for us to be effective in negotiation.

At the core of every human being is a fundamental need to feel valued. This need is present at the heart of every negotiation, where the underlying question, often unconsciously, being asked is: Am I being valued? Our quest for this validation influences not just our negotiations, but also our overall life experiences. Whether you consciously recognise it or not, this human need for validation is ever-present.

Our need to be valued is so strong that the fear of self-devaluation holds many of us back from negotiating effectively. This fear can take many forms, such as the fear of:

- seeming inappropriate

- being at a loss for words

- having insufficient information

- entering into potential conflict

- facing the unknown

- being rejected

- appearing incompetent

- losing a job or a deal

- not being acknowledged for our expertise and knowledge

- being judged and failing.

All these fears stem from our concerns about diminishing our own value. If we recognise that our need to be valued is a universal human need, we can more readily acknowledge, and accept, that the person we're negotiating with also likely shares these same concerns, and is likely to also be seeking the assurance of their value.

When I first started coaching, both individuals and teams, I was struck by moments of 'sonder'—the realisation that everyone is living their own rich life, with their own narrative that is as full of fears and concerns as our own. Knowing this, and understanding that we all share the same fundamental need to feel valued brought me a sense of unity. It's a reminder that, at the core of our human experience, we are all equal—something we often forget in the midst of a negotiation.

Our value isn't always equal

There are two fundamental sources of value, and they aren't always equal. It's important that you understand what these two sources of value are so that you don't mistakenly devalue yourself.

First, there's intrinsic value, which is deeply rooted within you. Think of this as your personal sense of worth, the regard you hold for yourself, your inner compass guiding your understanding of what you deserve and what you're capable of achieving. This intrinsic value is constant and unshakeable. When you are aware of and acknowledge your intrinsic value, you recognise it as the driving force behind your actions, empowering you to seek out opportunities that reflect your true worth.

On the other hand, extrinsic value is shaped by the world around us: by the market, societal norms, and various external metrics. This extrinsic value is fluid, changing with circumstances, such as your role, industry or location. Extrinsic value is influenced by factors like supply and demand, and it often reflects how others perceive our worth.

The extrinsic value you negotiate for, whether monetary or otherwise, is separate from your intrinsic value as a person. Negotiations revolve around specific terms; the extrinsic value you bring is determined by the benefit and usefulness of what you offer to the other party. However, remember that extrinsic value is not, and will never be, a measure of your intrinsic worth. Circumstances and context might affect the extrinsic value you receive, but this does not diminish your intrinsic value. Your intrinsic worth always remains constant and unchanged by external factors.

Over the years, I've seen friends and colleagues face involuntary redundancy, leading them to confuse the two sources of value. Many began to doubt their intrinsic worth, not realising that it was their extrinsic value to the organisation that had changed. The value (usefulness or benefits) they offered to their business was no longer required in the context of the organisation's immediate needs and interests. The environment around them changed, altering their extrinsic value to that organisation at that particular time.

As previously mentioned, our unconscious need to feel valued is ever-present. That's why understanding the interplay between these two sources of value is crucial, helping us avoid confusion between them. In every negotiation, it's vital to remember that our intrinsic worth is not what's being discussed. We are negotiating terms and conditions for an exchange of benefits, or extrinsic value, not our personal worth. Recognising this distinction is essential, allowing us to negotiate from a position of strength and clarity, and not from a place of fear.

This leads to an important point regarding negotiations, whether it's pricing for your business services, negotiating your salary or setting boundaries for your time. Successfully negotiating your extrinsic value starts with an unwavering belief in yourself. As Eleanor Roosevelt said, 'No-one can make you feel inferior without your consent.'

If you doubt your worth, if your sense of self, your intrinsic value, fluctuates, convincing others of your worth becomes a challenge. We set our own limits on what we believe is possible. Our intrinsic belief in ourself lays the foundation upon which our extrinsic achievements are built.

Believing in our intrinsic worth is critical, whether we're negotiating for ourself or our organisation. This belief not only empowers us in negotiations, but also ensures that external factors don't erode our sense of self. It prevents triggering our deep-seated need to feel valued, which can cloud our ability to recognise the extrinsic value available.

Case study: George charging his worth

George spent thirty years of his career working his way up the corporate ladder. With a natural gift for the gab, he had a knack for building relationships, which served him well in his sales

(continued)

and business development role. After years of outperforming and being recognised for consistently hitting and exceeding his numbers, his line manager changed, and George found himself working for someone who wanted to change the way he and the sales team operated, with a greater emphasis on process and systems and less focus on relationships.

His new line manager didn't value the way George worked, and instead of seeking to understand what support George needed to adapt to a new way forward, he berated him for being out of the office visiting customers when he expected him to be in the office updating the sales system. Over time, George's confidence and bubbly character diminished. The pressure from his new line manager to spend more time completing administrative duties was having an effect on his sense of self and the contribution he was making.

With his mental health deteriorating, he decided it was time to part ways with his line manager and to take some well-needed time to rest and reassess what he wanted. During this time, he completed qualifications in personal training and nutrition and decided to embark on a new career path outside of corporate. George had been into fitness since his late teens, and it was something he was deeply passionate about.

What was interesting was that, although he'd earned a high income in his sales career, he didn't know how to feel comfortable charging for his time in a training session, initially offering to train people for free or in exchange for a small nominal amount. His ability to charge reflected the lack of confidence in his own value, even though the value he brought to the table was significant, both in years of experience and knowledge.

He had a genuine care for the outcomes his clients wanted yet failed to realise that there needed to be an appropriate value exchange to reflect the results his clients wanted. On a cold rainy day, it would be easier for his clients to cancel a session that they had not paid for or had only paid a small amount of money for that they wouldn't miss. By charging less than his extrinsic market value, he was reducing the likelihood of the client getting the transformation they wanted because they didn't have enough skin in the game. George had priced his extrinsic value based on his doubt in his intrinsic value. He'd inadvertently let the perception of his previous line manager impact his sense of self-worth.

Thankfully, George partnered with a gym that asked him not to undercut the other personal trainers. It was the support he needed to enable him to charge his market value. He's still doing the inner work on recognising that, despite a bad experience with his previous manager, his intrinsic value was never on the table to be traded up or down.

Price, cost and value are not the same

Now that we understand we're never negotiating our intrinsic value, it's important to clarify some common confusions when it comes to negotiating extrinsic value. As I've mentioned previously, the concept of value is often misunderstood. So, what exactly is extrinsic value, and how is it determined?

In its simplest form, extrinsic value involves solving problems and creating solutions. It's a subjective measure, referring to the perceived benefit or usefulness of a product or service to the buyer. Value considers how well a product or service meets the needs or desires of an individual or business. It's not solely about the financial aspect; it encompasses the overall satisfaction and utility the buyer derives.

If we consider value as the anticipated impact of a solution in meeting a specific need, it helps us see why different people assign different values to the same item or service. The anticipated impact, and therefore value, of the product or service will vary based on the person's or group's need or desire for the offered solution.

In negotiations, many people tend to negotiate only on price or cost, confusing them with value. However, it's crucial to recognise that price and cost are distinctly different concepts.

Price is the most tangible and visible of the three. It's the specific figure a business sets for a product or service, evident on proposals, contracts or invoices. For instance, when your company purchases software, the price is the quoted amount for the licence. While price is often the focal point in negotiations, it's important to recognise that it isn't the sole factor.

Cost extends beyond the initial price. It encompasses all expenses involved in acquiring, implementing and maintaining the product or service. Taking the software example, the cost includes not just the purchase price of the licence, but also implementation fees, staff training, necessary hardware upgrades, and ongoing support and maintenance. Cost is a comprehensive measure, indicating the overall financial investment.

Value is about the perceived benefit or utility of a product or service. It leans more towards qualitative assessment rather than just quantitative figures. Take the software example: its value could be gauged by how well it streamlines operations, boosts employee productivity or improves customer satisfaction.

Value is a metric that encompasses the long-term impact and the return on investment, beyond just the initial expense. When we think about negotiations or making decisions, blending these concepts can be really powerful. It's about inquiring, 'Is this investment worthwhile? Does it align with our business or personal objectives? Are we gaining a significant return on our investment?' This holistic approach is essential for effective business strategies and informed personal purchasing decisions.

What do you truly value?

If value is the anticipated impact, usefulness or benefit of a prospective solution in meeting a need or a want, then understanding and identifying what you truly value is essential before entering any negotiation.

To illustrate this, let's consider a salary negotiation. The salary you receive is the price the company pays for your skills. However, the cost incurred for your work might include time spent commuting, travelling away from home, time away from your family, missing your children's school events or not being able to choose your downtime due to mandatory holidays during the company's Christmas shutdown. Understanding these trade-offs is crucial in evaluating the overall value of the salary package.

In considering value, it's imperative to think about the return on investment. As I previously mentioned, a common error is focusing solely on price in negotiations and mistaking it for value. But the reality is stark: no amount of money can compensate for missing significant life events, like the birth of a child or a family funeral, due to work commitments.

During salary negotiations, it's crucial not to overlook what truly brings fulfilment. It's easy to be swayed by apparent benefits like a high salary, company prestige or an ideal office location. Yet, these 'shiny things' might not equate to long-term happiness. It's important to remember that a hefty salary doesn't necessarily mean job satisfaction.

So, let's go deeper. Reflect on the role and its responsibilities. Ask yourself: which aspects of the job are likely to bring you true joy and satisfaction? Think about your preferred working style. How much freedom, flexibility and autonomy are essential for you? And don't forget to factor in your work-life balance.

Next, consider the leadership and team dynamics. What kind of support, recognition and opportunities for growth do you find valuable? How significant are camaraderie and meaningful connections at your workplace?

Then, turn your thoughts to the company culture. Identify the aspects of the organisational environment that would make you feel valued and supported. Look beyond the immediate team and consider the wider business community. Finally, evaluate the role itself. Determine what you find most valuable about it. Is it the title, the scope of responsibilities or perhaps something entirely different?

Beyond work, consider your personal goals. Ask yourself, what do you want in terms of family, lifestyle, finances, fitness, hobbies and self-improvement? Understanding these goals is crucial for knowing what you really value. Spend time thinking about these things. What makes you truly happy and satisfied? Identifying these values puts you in a better position to negotiate for what really counts.

This clear understanding goes beyond just salary talks. Knowing what you value enables you to match your job with your overall life goals, paving the way for a career that's not just profitable, but also fulfilling.

This idea applies when negotiating deals for your business too. How deep do you explore the value that your company is seeking? Are you thinking broader than the remit of your job role and function, and considering value at a holistic level for the organisation? Do you have a clear understanding of what other functions in the business deem valuable? Is there alignment between the internal functions?

If you know what your business values, then choosing the partners, suppliers and customers you work with also becomes significantly easier. If your business values high quality, then it won't be aligned to working with suppliers who are the cheapest on the market because they provide a lesser quality product. If your business values providing its customers the best user experience, then it's appropriate for you to carry these values into negotiations with suppliers.

By seeking suppliers that can meet your company's high standard for quality, and who understand and align with its vision for an exceptional user experience, you help your business live and breathe what it values through the supply chain. This maintains the integrity of the brand, builds the associated reputation of the business in the marketplace and creates a competitive advantage beyond price.

By identifying what your business values, your approach ensures that the outcomes of your negotiations contribute to the broader business goals and make decisions that align with its long-term objectives, not just short-term gains. Successful negotiation is not just about getting the lowest price, but about aligning with partners who can uphold and contribute to what we fundamentally value.

If we only concentrate on price, we miss the bigger picture. We might think we're saving money, but we could end up costing ourselves more and not getting as much value as we expected. As you think about your negotiations, are you identifying what you and your company truly value? Are you negotiating for value, or are you getting caught in price and cost discussions without considering the total return on investment for yourself and your company?

Identify what they truly value

Understanding what you and your business values is only half the journey. The next step is identifying what the other party in the negotiation values. This knowledge is crucial for finding mutual interests, determining what's negotiable and establishing the necessary value exchange.

Who are you negotiating with? Refer to the stakeholders you identified in Chapter 4. In salary negotiations, for example, this could involve a recruiter, a hiring manager or a HR manager. In a business example, this could involve the CFO and the supply chain operations director, each of whom will have different priorities and values. It's your job to map out these values as accurately as possible.

You may not have all the answers right away, but you can make educated guesses and then validate them through conversations and interviews. The more precisely you understand what the other party values as well as their needs and interests, the more effectively you can negotiate.

Failing to grasp what the other party values can severely hinder your ability to position your offerings in light of their needs. Likewise, a lack of understanding about their values can limit your success in achieving what you want in return.

Perception is their reality

In any negotiation, both parties aim to maximise their received value. However, the real challenge isn't just understanding our own values and those of the other person. The crucial task is effectively packaging our value and aligning our offerings with the other party's needs. For example, if you're negotiating for a new role that requires a security clearance or clearance to work with children and you already possess these qualifications, you can highlight this as part of your value proposition. Emphasise how your existing clearances not only showcase your skills but also provide additional benefits to the organisation, such as cost savings, reduced administrative burden and a faster onboarding process.

If we can't communicate our value in a way that resonates with the other party, they're unlikely to be interested, diminishing our chances of maximising the return we seek. While it's important to focus on what we say and do at the negotiation table, if we wait until we're at the table to shape the other party's perception of our value, it's already too late. Influencing how our value is perceived needs to happen well before sitting down to negotiate. If you are a job candidate applying for a competitive position, you can influence the employer's perception of your value even before the interview by actively engaging on professional networks like LinkedIn. This ensures you create a strong personal brand that demonstrates your value and expertise, increasing the perception of your value in the employer's mind, and increasing your chances of securing favourable terms.

In today's interconnected world, the concept of six degrees of separation might now be closer to two or three. Consequently, people, whether employers, clients, suppliers, colleagues or competitors, will form opinions about us, our value or the value our business brings long before we meet them. Whether these perceptions enhance or diminish our value in their eyes, is ultimately up to us. The choice lies with us: do we want to consciously influence the perception they hold?

We can't hide, but we can influence perception.

Leaving your counterparts' perception of your value to chance risks them not recognising your true value. To create more valuable agreements for ourselves and others, we must be intentional. Proactively shaping how we're perceived is not just an option; it's a strategic necessity in navigating the complexities of our professional and personal interactions. This might mean starting a blog to showcase your expertise in your industry, updating your social media profiles with tips, industry trends and case studies of successful projects. When clients research you before reaching out, they already have a positive impression of your skills and value, making them more likely to agree to your terms and perceive you as a top-tier performer.

We have different levels of awareness

One of the most common challenges in being human is that we all see the world differently, and our perception is limited to what we are exposed to. Time and again in negotiations, I've observed individuals and teams making assumptions that the other party shares their view of value. They expect that others will inherently understand the logic of their perspective and the proposals they present.

However, these assumptions often lead to a lack of awareness about what the other party truly needs, resulting in missed opportunities to demonstrate value. Entering a negotiation requires an understanding of a problem that needs solving, or a desire or need that must be fulfilled. Imagine a catering company pitching its services to a corporate client planning a series of high-profile events. The catering company assumes that the client will be impressed by their gourmet menu options and exclusive partnerships with top chefs, but the client is more concerned with reliability and scalability. Because the caterer focuses on pitching the gourmet aspects, the client doesn't see how their need for efficient service will be met. The caterer failed to understand the client's priorities, so they didn't highlight their logistical capabilities and experience with large events.

This misunderstanding is the most common reason people confuse selling and negotiating as the same thing. In reality, I can't negotiate a deal with you unless you have interest in buying what I'm selling. The subtle yet important distinction to remember is that selling or marketing involve creating interest for your product or service, while negotiating is about agreeing on the terms of the deal once it's established that the other party has an interest in what you're offering. (Refer back to Chapter 5 about first determining if the conditions exist for negotiation.)

When it comes to creating interest, there are five levels of awareness:

1. Unaware

2. Problem aware

3. Solution aware

4. Product aware

5. Most aware.

To illustrate this, let's consider a familiar scenario at home. Suppose you're eager to plan a family holiday. However, your partner, who runs their own business, might not immediately align with you on the need, destination, budget or timing.

At first, your partner, content with the usual routine, may not see the need for a holiday. This is the *unaware* stage, where there's no recognition of the need for a change. Meanwhile, you notice stress in the family, the mundane nature of daily life or the long gap since your last trip away.

By bringing these issues to light, you shift your partner to the *problem aware* stage, where they recognise a need for stress relief or family bonding. This doesn't mean they're ready to 'buy' a family holiday, but in getting them to recognise a need (see a problem) you can build interest for a solution.

In building interest for a solution, the suggestion of a family trip, you move your partner from problem aware to the *solution aware* stage, as they begin to see the benefits of a potential holiday. When you propose specific ideas, such as a beach resort or a mountain cabin, your partner becomes *product aware*.

Finally, presenting a detailed holiday plan, with the destination, itinerary and budget in mind, brings your partner to the *most aware* stage, where they fully comprehend and appreciate the proposed solution.

Now that both of you have reached the most aware stage, more effective negotiation of the holiday details becomes possible. Your partner might raise issues concerning budget or timing, and you'll work together to negotiate a solution that suits you both.

In this home scenario, as in our business negotiations, it's important to realise the other party might not start with the same awareness level or perspective. Successfully navigating from the initial awareness stage to achieving full alignment is crucial in any negotiation.

Before you can negotiate terms effectively, you must understand the other party's awareness level, needs and interests. As you guide the other party from being unaware to most aware, your role evolves from educating and influencing to negotiating an agreement.

In the journey of having conversations to reach agreement, you will need to create interest (sell) to ensure the conditions are present for the negotiation. Sometimes this happens at multiple points through the journey to agreement. This is particularly noticeable in the solution aware and product aware stages. Here, while you're still creating interest (by emphasising benefits or unique features), you may start preliminary negotiations, especially if the other party starts inquiring or discussing the terms.

Whether in business or personal scenarios, our objective is to help people recognise value so that it can be effectively exchanged. That can only happen if we understand where their awareness levels are, and we meet them where they are before we lead them to where we, and they, want to go.

How are we exchanging value?

The primary goal in a negotiation is the exchange of value. Essentially, you provide what I value, and I offer what you value in return. This exchange reaches its maximum potential when I give you something you perceive as highly valuable at a low cost to me, and similarly, you offer me something I perceive highly valuable, with minimal cost to you. The ideal scenario is where both parties receive high perceived value while incurring the lowest possible costs, thereby maximising the value for both.

However, this objective isn't always straightforward. Different negotiation styles can lead to varying behaviours. For instance, if we are negotiating with someone driven by their emotional Joker, the exchange might not be as logical or rational. Furthermore, as we've just discussed, the awareness levels of the parties play a crucial role. If someone is unaware of a problem, the value you offer might not be fully appreciated or understood.

Given this complexity, multiple approaches are possible in the exchange of value. On one end of the spectrum, we find the less desirable methods, such as destroying, taking or simply protecting value. On the more positive end, there are approaches like giving, sharing, creating and growing value. While I've delineated these seven outcomes as distinct, they are interrelated and can impact each other.

- *Destroying value* occurs when we become adversarial, with each party focusing on their gains at the expense of the other. It's most commonly seen when one party excessively focuses on price without considering the other party's needs, causing the deal to fall apart.

- *Taking value* happens when one party gains more at the other's expense—a classic win-lose situation. Employing aggressive tactics to secure a much lower price might benefit you short term, but could strain or end the relationship, jeopardising future opportunities.

- *Protecting value* is about ensuring the deal stays above a certain benefit threshold for you. Often, I see teams and businesses so focused on not losing what they have, that they neglect to explore how value could be created in other ways.

- *Giving value* could involve concessions or benefits that don't significantly impact your position but greatly improve the deal for the other party, building goodwill and trust, potentially leading to more favourable future agreements.

- *Sharing value* might see each side conceding on some points to gain more on others, leading to a more advantageous agreement for all involved.

- *Creating value* involves finding ways to 'expand the cake' before slicing it. This approach identifies shared interests or complementary needs, crafting solutions that are more beneficial collectively than separately.

- *Growing value* is about continually seeking ways to enhance the deal's worth. This could mean regular reviews of the agreement to adjust terms, add services or adapt to changing circumstances, ensuring that the deal remains valuable and relevant.

Now that we've defined the different approaches in the exchange of value, let's explore how these methods work together, impacting negotiation outcomes either positively or negatively.

Creating and sharing value usually work together. In negotiations, when you come up with a unique solution that adds new value, like a new product or service, it often leads to sharing that value.

Giving and protecting value might look like opposites, but they can work together. Sometimes, giving a bit in a negotiation, like a small concession, is a smart move to protect your bigger interests. It's a tactical play to know when to give a little to safeguard the overall deal.

Taking and destroying value, unfortunately, can happen at the same time. If one party is too aggressive in a negotiation, like pushing for very low prices, it can backfire. This kind of approach can ruin the relationship or cause long-term issues, destroying the value for everyone involved.

Growing and sharing value, when value increases in a deal, often leads to both sides benefiting. For instance, in a long-term deal with a supplier, making things more efficient or improving quality isn't just good for one side, it grows the value for both, turning it into a shared benefit.

Negotiation isn't just about what you gain, it's how you balance different approaches to create, grow and share value. Effective negotiation is about smart value exchange—knowing what strategy to apply when and how to work towards deals that everyone can feel good about.

How do you know what behavioural strategy to use when?

Now that you're familiar with how value can be exchanged, let's explore two effective negotiation strategies for maximising it: competing (to claim or capture value) and collaborating (to create value). In Chapter 3, we discussed that being effective at negotiation means being able to switch between both competitive and collaborative styles when the situation calls for it. Knowing when to be competitive and when to be collaborative can significantly improve your negotiation outcomes.

The key factor in choosing your negotiation strategy often lies in the importance of the relationship beyond the current deal. We all have long memories and, given our deep need to feel valued, we often remember the interactions that leave us feeling less than valued far more acutely than the interactions that do make us feel valued. It's, therefore, imperative that we consider the impact of any chosen negotiation strategy on the relationship before deciding which approach to take.

In scenarios where our interaction with the other party is a one-time occurrence, or very limited, a competitive strategy may be less harmful. Competitive approaches are fitting in situations where trust isn't a crucial element of the deal, such as when interactions are limited to a single agreement. These strategies are typically used when the 'cake' is fixed in size and the focus is on claiming the largest possible share. This type of situation is typically where we see The General archetype most effective. Their focus is on taking more value than they give in exchange because there is only a fixed amount of cake and it's a zero-sum game environment. This is often the case in negotiations that are primarily driven by price, where other factors play a minimal role. In these situations, the emphasis is less on building a lasting relationship and more on the immediate benefit of the deal. However, it's crucial to weigh these approaches carefully, as they may not be suitable for negotiations that involve ongoing interactions or require the nurturing of trust and cooperation.

Using a transactional, competitive approach, like The General archetype, with someone you deal with regularly likely won't sustain the relationship over time. In negotiations where the relationship is expected to exist beyond the deal, competitive tactics can quickly erode any trust.

But if your dealings are transactional, then a competitive strategy might work better. What's really important to understand is that being transactional doesn't mean being unprofessional, rude or disrespectful — that behaviour rarely gets any agreement. Being transactional simply means that building trust, and the depth of the relationship, isn't your primary focus. Professionalism is still key, but the emphasis is more on the specifics of the deal outcome rather than the relationship, especially when the relationship isn't expected to continue beyond the transaction.

If the relationship is of great importance, likely to exist beyond the deal, and there is an opportunity to expand the cake (create value), then the collaborative strategy is more appropriate. The Diplomat archetype will be the one that maximises value in this scenario.

Your strategy isn't always in your control

One certainty in negotiations is that your strategy and approach must adapt to your counterpart. At the start of my workshops, participants often think it's easier to negotiate with an amateur negotiator than a professional; however, by the end, they usually see the benefits of dealing with a professional.

Why? The success of your negotiation largely hinges on the other party's willingness and skill level. Negotiating with amateurs can be unpredictable. It's like playing a game where the other player doesn't fully grasp the rules or has a unique approach. While this can sometimes work in your favour, perhaps if they are The Accommodator archetype, more often than not, it limits the potential outcomes because the other party can't or won't match your level of negotiation intelligence. A lack of willingness is one hurdle, but insufficient skill on their part presents a different set of challenges altogether. It's difficult to create value and optimise the deal together if the other party doesn't have the skill.

The best case here is that both parties adopt The Dealer archetype where they give and take but settle for a middle ground. The two sides will be unable to access the optimal value that could be exchanged if both parties had the skills to discover it.

Negotiation nuggets:
V — Identify your value

- *Understanding intrinsic and extrinsic value*: Recognise the difference between unchangeable intrinsic value (your personal self-worth) and fluctuating extrinsic value (how the outside world values your contributions). Keeping this distinction in mind is vital for your own confidence and can prevent you from conflating your worth with external evaluations.

- *Overcoming fear in negotiations*: Acknowledge that fear often stems from concerns about our value being diminished. The other party likely shares the same fears. Acknowledge the human need to feel valued, and focus your efforts on solving problems and creating solutions that meet the needs of others, increasing your extrinsic value.

- *Price, cost and value*: Price is what you pay, cost is the total expense involved, and value is the benefit derived from a product or service. Understanding these distinctions helps ascertain the true worth of what you're negotiating.

- *Identifying personal and counterparty values*: It's crucial to know not just what you value, but also what the other party values. This knowledge is key to crafting proposals that resonate and lead to mutually beneficial outcomes.

- *Perception management*: Early influence over how others perceive your value is essential. By shaping perceptions before negotiations begin, you can improve the likelihood of a successful exchange.

- *Awareness levels*: Adjust your negotiation approach based on the other party's level of awareness from unaware to most aware. This helps in aligning both parties' understanding and expectations.

- *Approaches to value exchange*: Be aware of various value exchange methods, like creating, sharing, giving, protecting, taking, destroying and growing value, and use them strategically.

- *Choosing negotiation strategies*: Decide when to apply competitive versus collaborative value exchange strategies based on the relationship and context. This choice impacts both immediate outcomes and long-term interactions.

Focus five action list: Identify the value

Action	Activity	Done
Understand your intrinsic value	Acknowledge your inherent worth and ensure it stays distinct from external factors in any negotiation.	
Determine extrinsic value	Assess the extrinsic value of what you offer by considering the benefits and impact on the other party.	
Clarify what you truly value	Identify your non-negotiables and what matters most to you, both personally and professionally.	
Research what the other party values	Understand the needs, desires and priorities of your negotiation counterparts to align your offers effectively.	
Communicate your value effectively	Present your value proposition clearly and compellingly, emphasising benefits that meet the other party's needs.	

Chapter 8

A — Analyse the data

The second key to value is to analyse the data. I know this can conjure up many different images in people's minds; for me, it used to be numbers, nerds and spreadsheets—now, it's a lot broader! I think of people, their stories, perspectives, beliefs and much more—it's like piecing together a puzzle. What images come to mind for you?

Gathering and analysing data is a fundamental part of the planning and preparation process for negotiations, and the omission of this stage is why so many people are underprepared for the conversations they need to have. I understand. It all can feel a little too hard and complex, and it's easy to become overwhelmed by the thought of where to start and choose to wing it instead.

When you consider the images that come to mind when you think about data, were they conducive to you wanting to 'analyse' the data or did it make you want to run a mile?

To make this process enjoyable and straightforward, I'll cover the types of data you need to collect, how to use it and what mistakes to avoid, as well as how to capture, store and share data appropriately. My goal is to simplify this process and make it an accessible key to unlocking value.

In case you hadn't already spotted, you just completed your first exercise in gathering and analysing the data. You identified the images that came to your mind, and you interpreted whether those images were conducive to you wanting to 'analyse the data' or avoid doing it. You now have information, it's what you do with it that counts.

Information equals power

You've probably heard the phrase, 'information equals power'. It also most likely conjured images of information that can be used against you, or that you could use against another party. In Chapter 9 we will talk about power and how to use it, but for now, I want you to understand that information is not just a source of power, it's also a source of confidence. This confidence is crucial for having the necessary conversations to achieve the value you want and deserve.

The objective of analysing the data is to transform it into confidence. The essence of this chapter is understanding the importance of focusing your efforts on gathering the right information because confidence stems from being well-informed, leading to conversations that are both necessary and effective.

The three stages of negotiation

Before we dive into analysing the data, it would be remiss of me to not flag that there are three fundamental stages in a negotiation where analysing the data is applicable.

1. Pre-negotiation

This stage involves preparation, deal design and set-up, and is where 80 per cent of your negotiation efforts should be focused. The success of your negotiation hinges on this phase. By analysing information sources, understanding your leverage and recognising your value, you can plan and rehearse your approach, making the actual negotiation process much smoother.

2. During negotiation

Often, too much emphasis is placed on this phase. While the tactics and responses during the negotiation are important, they should not be your only focus. We'll go through what kinds of data you should be analysing in this phase.

3. Post-negotiation

This stage involves reflection and analysis of the negotiation process and outcomes. Don't underestimate the importance of this phase: it's easy to start celebrating or commiserating, but the key here is not about whether you think you succeeded or failed, it's about what you learned that will help you level up even further next time.

We'll discuss more about what else you need to do in these three stages in the execute your plan stage.

There are only two sources of data

To keeps things simple, I want you to know there are only two sources of data: people and published. There are multiple ways to subdivide this in a more complex way, but I've found it doesn't really help too much other than to cause massive overwhelm.

What is people data?

When you gather information from people, it's not just through formal interviews or structured discussions, it's also from everyday conversations, the casual exchanges about someone's weekend and interests, and the little things you notice about how they behave and react. This kind of information is valuable. It gives you insight into who the person is, what they think, feel, believe and how they see things around them. For example, in casual conversation, a counterparty mentions their involvement in community service and their passion for working with and advocating for disadvantaged groups. This information reveals what they value, which enables you to tailor your approach. By emphasising how your proposal benefits the wider business and community and is equitable for both parties, you make your proposal more appealing to that person.

Your own intuition, experience and human judgement is also people data, and is especially valuable in situations where data is incomplete or misleading. Don't underestimate the power of your own 'Spidey sense'—what your intuition picked up that you haven't consciously allowed yourself to acknowledge.

People data also includes sources such as personal social media. When people post their thoughts and experiences online, they're often sharing personal and subjective information. It's the stories and perspectives that everyone shares that add context and depth to your understanding of who they are and what is valuable to them.

In negotiations, people data is about getting the deeper insights that go beyond just the facts and figures. Understanding why someone thinks or acts a certain way can help make a significant difference to positioning the value you want to exchange.

What is published data?

Published data encompasses virtually any recorded or documented information, regardless of its format. This includes everything from traditional media, such as books, research papers and reports, to digital content, such as websites, online databases and articles.

Published data opens a world of perspectives, often providing a more objective view that enriches our understanding. This data can be concrete and measurable—think market trends, specific reports or relevant statistics on the gender pay gap and the diversity on company boards. It also includes insights that are more subjective, such as a CEO's analysis of company performance in an annual report or their predictions about upcoming market trends.

Published doesn't necessarily mean widely disseminated; it also applies to data compiled and recorded within a company, whether shared publicly or kept private.

How might access to this type of data influence your own decisions or insights in your negotiations?

Why people data matters

In negotiations, the importance of people data really can't be overstated. Without understanding the people you're negotiating with, it's like walking into a room blindfolded—you're essentially navigating in the dark.

At the negotiation table, people data is the insights you gain from what they say, how they act and even what they don't say. Think about the last time you were in a negotiation or any kind of important discussion. Remember how much you could infer from the other person's tone, their body language or the way they chose their words? That's the value in people data. It's not just about the raw information they provide, but also about the subtleties that surround it.

Let's suppose you're trying to negotiate a deal or a salary. Knowing the factual data, like market rates and financial trends, is necessary, but understanding the person sitting across from you is equally, if not more, important. Their motivations, pressures and preferences can dramatically steer the course of your negotiation.

For instance, imagine you're a consultant negotiating the roll out of a new ERP (enterprise resource planning) system with a cross-functional team led by Leila. Through team meetings and informal conversations, you've learned that Leila highly values thoroughness and precision but is under significant pressure from senior management to accelerate the rollout to meet the end-of-financial-year deadline. Knowing this, you could suggest a staggered rollout, where critical modules are implemented first to meet the deadline, while also allowing time for thorough integration of other features. By addressing Leila's need for precision and the urgency from senior management, you can make the proposal more compelling and aligned with her priorities.

But gathering people data isn't just about being strategic, it's also about building connections and trust. People are more likely to strike a deal with someone they like, that they feel understands them and they can relate to. And for that, you need to really listen and observe, to connect not just on a business level, but on a human level too.

So, when you're preparing for your next negotiation, remember to pay as much attention to the people, including your own 'Spidey sense', as you do to the numbers. It's this balance between understanding the hard facts and the human elements that often leads to the most successful outcomes.

And that, in a nutshell, is the power of people data.

◆ ◆ ◆

Earlier in Chapter 4, we talked about who matters in a negotiation. Now, it's about identifying them in your stakeholder map and determining not only what information you can get about them, but also what information they have that would help you. Also, think broader and consider who else could provide you insights on the people you've identified on your stakeholder map. You'll need to learn a lot about them to understand how they think, feel and act. What are they like when they are calm and relaxed? What do you know about their stress response and their mode of operandi under pressure? What will cause their Joker to take a seat at the table?

It all comes back to what they value extrinsically or their deeper intrinsic need to be valued. Consider what information you need to gather to give you more understanding about those areas.

Why published data matters

When we're gearing up for negotiations, whether it's for a contract renewal, a new partnership or a salary discussion, the role of published data is equally as crucial. It's a resource we can't afford to overlook. In the planning stage, this data serves as a backbone for our strategy. For instance, having access to annual reports, industry benchmarks, salary surveys or market analysis reports can give you a significant edge. It lets you know where you stand and what is realistic to aim for.

When you sit down at the negotiating table, you want to be armed with more than just your own expectations and demands. You need hard facts about what's appropriate, what's competitive and what could be achievable. Published data provides this information. It's not just about having the numbers; it's about understanding the landscape.

Also, in negotiations, credibility is key. When you back up your points with data from respected sources, it strengthens your position. It shows you're not just coming from a place of personal interest, but from a place of informed understanding.

Then there's anticipating and countering the other party's arguments. If you know the common trends and data points in your industry, you can prepare for what the other party might bring up and have your responses ready. Understanding this is like getting the lay of the land before starting a big project.

Data also help you to set targets that are ambitious, yet achievable, based on actual market conditions. It's one thing to aim high in a negotiation, but it's important you sense check to ensure your goals are grounded in reality to avoid making yourself look like you've been smoking something you shouldn't have!

Negotiations often involve uncovering opportunities for mutual benefit. Armed with solid data, you can more effectively pinpoint areas where joint value can be created. This not only clarifies your position, but also gives insight into the other party's perspective, opening doors to solutions that benefit both sides.

In any setting where negotiation is involved, gathering and analysing the appropriate published data as part of your preparation will make a significant difference. It's about being informed, credible and strategic, all of which are key to building confidence and successful negotiation outcomes.

Analyse the data through multiple lenses

Even when data has been gathered and analysed, I've seen a lot of negotiators unravel because their analysis was only done from one perspective: their own.

We talked about perception in Chapter 7, and in business and life, perspectives matter and that doesn't just mean our own. If we only look at the negotiation through our own lens, we're going to fail to create maximum value. It's also much harder to have our position hold weight if we can't demonstrate that we've considered the other party's position.

When it comes to analysing the data, there are three lenses I want you to look through: yours, theirs and as an outsider looking down on the situation.

If it helps, set up your room with three different chairs and assign a chair for each perspective. Sit in each different chair and notice what you see. It's a powerful exercise to help you stay present with the various perspectives that will be in the room. Say you're negotiating a supplier contract for your company. You've gathered data on the supplier's pricing, delivery options and the quality of their products. Now in preparation for your negotiation, you analyse the data through three lenses:

Your lens: From your perspective, you want to secure the best possible price, ensure timely delivery and maintain high product quality. You're also interested in negotiating favourable payment terms to help with cashflow management.

Their lens: Now, sit in the second chair and view the situation from the supplier's perspective. They might be concerned about maintaining a healthy profit margin, securing long-term clients and ensuring timely payments. They could also be dealing with their own supply chain challenges and cost pressures.

Outsider's lens: Finally take the outsider's perspective. Imagine you're a neutral third party observing this negotiation. What would you notice about the interaction between the two of you? You might see that both sides have valid concerns and goals. There might be an opportunity for a compromise, such as agreeing on a slightly higher price in exchange for more flexible payment terms if cashflow is of greater priority. Alternatively, you may suggest the supplier give you a lower price in exchange for a long-term contract, meeting their need for stability.

Taking time to consider different perspectives leads to more effective negotiation conversations and outcomes. Proposals become more robust because they consider each party's needs and interests, and relationships are less likely to be strained due to greater empathy and understanding.

Now that you know what the two data sources are, why they matter and the different perspectives you need to consider when analysing the data, we'll look at the practical uses of both people and published data in negotiations.

The practical use of people data in negotiations

When we're planning a negotiation, the key is to apply people data effectively. It's a straightforward concept: we gather insights not only from what is said during meetings, but from every interaction, observing and listening closely.

In practise, this means focusing on the finer details. When we're determining what someone really wants from a negotiation, it's not just about listening to their words. We need to pay attention to the stories they share, the concerns they voice, and especially to what they're not saying directly. These clues reveal their true motivations and can be incredibly valuable. Let's say you're in a partnership negotiation, and your client repeatedly emphasises cost savings but also briefly mentions the company's struggle with employee turnover and the need for a supportive work environment. These comments suggest their true concern might be employee satisfaction and retention, not just costs. By addressing these underlying concerns and proposing cost-effective measures alongside initiatives to enhance workplace culture, you demonstrate understanding and commitment to providing value. By reading between the lines, you can uncover valuable insights for more effective negotiations.

Build rapport and relationships

Building a good rapport is crucial. As Simone Weil said, 'Attention is the rarest and purest form of generosity'. If you can find a way to connect with the other party and understand their perspective, the negotiation often goes more smoothly. This means finding common ground or, at the very least, understanding their standpoint to navigate the conversation better.

Some tips for building rapport include:

- *Active listening:* Show a genuine interest in what the other party is saying and reflect back what you hear to demonstrate your understanding.

- *Find common interests:* Common interests could be related to work, hobbies, sport or recent events. Shared interests can create a sense of camaraderie.

- *Personalise the conversation:* Use the other person's name and, if you've met them previously, refer to details they have shared to show you remember and value your interaction with them.

- *Be sincere:* We can sense when someone is going through the motions of small talk, which can be worse than getting straight to business. Be yourself, show genuine curiosity and empathy to build stronger relationships.

Planning and presenting proposals

Setting realistic expectations is also part of using people data effectively. Knowing what is within realistic parameters for the other party to commit to helps in forming a negotiation strategy that is both realistic and achievable. If the person you're talking to is not the final decision-maker, don't expect them to make the decision; prior to the negotiation, find out who is the decision-maker and, where possible, set up an information gathering meeting with them to understand their needs.

Consider the challenges they might be facing. If you understand these, you can position your proposal as a solution that fits their needs in ways they might not have anticipated. This strengthens your position in the negotiation. Tailoring your approach based on your understanding of the other party can be a game changer, demonstrating that you're offering something that resonates with their specific needs instead of presenting generic solutions.

Let's look at an example. You're negotiating with the head of operations at a manufacturing company about your logistics software. Through an information gathering meeting, you discover the company struggles with coordinating their supply chain efficiently, leading to delays and increased costs. The procurement team, unaware of these logistical issues, focuses solely on sourcing materials at the lowest cost without considering the impact on overall operations. When presenting your proposal, you highlight how your software addresses these problems by providing real-time tracking, improving deliveries and integrating procurement with operations to improve overall efficiency, rather than simply presenting the generic features and benefits of your software. By demonstrating a deep understanding of their unique situation, you build trust and position yourself as a valuable partner, making your proposal more compelling and strengthening your leverage in the negotiation.

Anticipating responses and objections

Predicting responses also becomes easier when you know the person you're negotiating with. If you're familiar with their style and how they've reacted in the past, you can plan your approach more effectively. People are often creatures of habit, so it's helpful to anticipate their next move and be ready for it.

In unfamiliar territory, we need a map, so don't overlook the importance of the wider network and relationships (people and published data) surrounding the person you're negotiating with. Use the resources available to give you insights into where to push and where to be cautious.

Lastly, anticipating objections is crucial. If you've done your homework and understand their concerns and priorities, you can be prepared to address their objections effectively. An important point to note: If your counterpart raises an issue, it's an objection. However, if you raise that same issue in anticipation of them objecting to it, it becomes a conversation point. Take the lead—don't be shy in addressing their concerns. It's better to have the issue be a conversation point than an objection. For example, if you anticipate a challenge on budget, address it proactively; for example, 'Many of our clients initially don't have a budget allocated for this work, but once they start working with us and see the value we provide, they find it's a worthwhile investment.'

You already do this more than you realise

If you think back to the family holiday you were planning on page 149, you're now negotiating with your partner and children about the destination. By paying attention to your family's past holiday preferences, their reactions to certain activities and their subtle hints about what they enjoy, you tailor your proposal to appeal to everyone.

Maybe your partner loves historical sites and your kids are excited about beaches. By using this people data, you find Dubrovnik (which is a great choice by the way!), a coastal city rich in history, pleasing everyone and making the negotiation smooth.

Whether at home or at work, if you don't take the time to get into the heads of the other party by gathering and analysing data about them, it's highly unlikely you'll get the outcome you want.

The practical use of published data in negotiation

When we get into the negotiations, the effective use of published data becomes a fundamental part of our approach. This isn't just about piling up a lot of data, it's about strategically using the information we have to improve our negotiation position.

Imagine you're preparing for a crucial negotiation; for example, let's say you're negotiating a price reduction. Before you even enter the room, you've immersed yourself in the relevant published data. Having in-depth information about commodity prices, market trends, competitive analysis and consumer behaviour doesn't just give you figures, it provides you with a narrative about the current market situation and where it might be heading. This insight is crucial in framing your offer and understanding the scope of the negotiation.

Using this data goes beyond adding substance to your arguments. When you reference data from credible sources, you're not just making a point, you're substantiating it with evidence. This adds a layer of authority to your position, making your arguments more compelling. Knowledge lays the groundwork for your negotiation strategy, giving you a solid base to operate from.

Future proof your position

Published data is invaluable in predicting and preparing for future trends. In negotiations, this means crafting proposals that are not just beneficial now, but also in the future. A lot of people don't connect the dots that if their salary isn't at least going up with inflation, their financial position is going backwards each year—and that's not even taking into consideration any performance-related increases. When negotiating a salary in a new job, published data may help you understand what is appropriate considering future inflation trends. You're looking at the long-term implications of today's decisions, ensuring that your negotiation strategy is forward-thinking.

Risk assessment is another area where published data proves essential. By analysing market fluctuations, consumer patterns and regulatory shifts, you can pinpoint potential risks and plan accordingly. This proactive approach ensures that your strategy is not only assertive, but also robust and adaptable. This could be appropriate at home when it comes to, for example, proactively negotiating your mortgage rates with your bank ahead of anticipated rate increases to protect yourself from being financially over extended.

This data-driven approach helps you save money and ensures that you are meeting the specific needs of your family at times when there could be a lot of uncertainty.

Using published data in your negotiation strategy helps you make your approach more accurate and informed. It allows you to negotiate based on solid facts, not just guesses. This change turns your negotiations from simple conversations into more strategic and thoughtful decision-making. It also will boost your confidence and make you a more effective negotiator.

Case study: The cost of undiscovered data

Sometimes we think we've done all the right things, but later find out we missed crucial data. That was the situation for Isaiah when he negotiated his salary for a new role he was taking. At the time, he was making a career change, moving out of finance into an operational role with a new company. He researched the salary level benchmark and, recognising that he didn't have proven experience in operations, negotiated and accepted a salary $10 000 lower than his current one. He expected that he'd be able to make this up by proving himself in the role and increasing his salary at the next pay review, which he understood from HR happened annually.

Six months after joining the business, Isaiah found out that the annual salary review process happens in mid-March. Because he joined in April, he wouldn't qualify for a pay review until he'd been with the company for a minimum of one year, which meant that his salary would be reviewed the following March — nearly two years after he joined. The only way an out-of-cycle review would be considered is if the managing director signed it off. Dejected, Isaiah was left with a decision: stay and incur a two-year wait before his salary was reviewed or consider looking elsewhere.

His experience highlights the importance of thoroughly understanding all aspects of the agreement, as missing crucial data can lead to unintended, long-lasting consequences. Isaiah recognised the power of asking questions about the terms and conditions of an agreement, and that these rules are often written to serve the interests of the party drafting them. By proactively asking the questions (however uncomfortable), he could have chosen whether to accept the terms or seek to negotiate.

How to use the data you've gathered for negotiation preparation

I want to step you through how to effectively use both people and published data to prepare for a negotiation. This step is crucial in turning any raw information you have into actionable insights and increasing your confidence for successful negotiations.

Pre-negotiation

In this stage, you are establishing the essential groundwork for the negotiation. By gaining a deep understanding of the following five key elements, you are making sure you are well-prepared and ready to think ahead strategically.

Walk-away points

- *Your limits:* Through a detailed analysis of both people and relevant published data, identify your limits. What can't you do, what can you do and what's not even on the table for discussion. Identifying your limits includes understanding the most acceptable terms for you and under what conditions you'd walk away from the deal.

- *Their limits:* Assess the other party's potential limits by analysing previous negotiations, market trends and their behavioural patterns. While you won't know for sure what their limits are, it's important to have a hypothesis that you can seek to validate in the negotiation itself.

Opening offers

- *Your initial proposal:* Develop your initial offer grounded in a comprehensive analysis of relevant data, ensuring it's ambitious, yet realistic, and is ultimately negotiable. Remember you can't get 100 per cent of what you want if you always start by asking for less. Note—in a complex negotiation involving numerous variables or levers it is not advisable to open ambitiously on every single lever. This approach can overwhelm and put the other party offside. Instead, prioritise key levers and present a balanced proposal that will allow for a constructive dialogue.

- *Their expected offer:* Predict the other party's opening offer by examining their negotiation history and current market conditions. They will likely open ambitiously too.

Stakeholder analysis

- *Mapping stakeholders:* Identify key players in the negotiation, using people and published data to understand their roles and influences. This may start with insights from existing relationships, identifying who the senior management team are through company websites or a Google search. Refer back to Chapter 4 for a refresher.

- *Interests and objections:* Leverage both data types to grasp the motivations, interests and potential objections of these stakeholders. This could be evident from their public statements, past actions and any available documentation or insights from those familiar with them.

Time pressures

- *Assessing time factors:* Acknowledge any time-sensitive elements that could affect the negotiation, such as impending deadlines.

- *Impact on negotiation:* Reflect on how these time constraints may shape your strategy and the strategy of the other party. Think back to the way the procurement manager on page 105 used their people data as leverage by understanding the supplier's timeline pressure.

Alternative options

- *Your NBOs (next best option):* Based on thorough data analysis, determine your most viable alternative plan if you don't reach a deal with this party.

- *Their NBOs:* Gauge the other party's alternatives, understanding their negotiation leverage and flexibility.

As you transition from preparation to the actual negotiation, your focus shifts from analysing the data to applying the data. This is where you bring your insights into play, adapting them to the real-time dynamics of negotiation.

During the negotiation

In this stage, you'll need to manoeuvre based on the evolving landscape, using your data insights to guide your decisions and adapt your strategies. You're still gathering and analysing data, but now you are doing it in real time. Here are some key things you'll need to keep in mind.

Adapting to responses

You're going to get data through the discussions that will require you to dynamically adjust your strategy during the negotiation. How you adapt will be informed by your deep understanding of stakeholder dynamics and the limits that you prepared pre-negotiation. Be careful not to go off-piste in the moment—use your data to anchor you.

Awareness of time pressures

When you feel the pressure of time, it's easy forget all the robust data you prepared in advance. Be aware of any time constraints during the negotiation as well as the broader context outside it. Use this knowledge to stay focused and efficient without letting time pressure be used against you. The best way to manage this is to prepare and align on an agenda for the key points that need to be discussed in advance and stick to it during the negotiation. If external deadlines or pressures are influencing the negotiation, acknowledge this data but don't let it dictate your pace or cause you to abandon your planned approach. Maintain control over the negotiation process; don't let time steer your actions.

Opportunity for value creation

Drawing on your insights from both people and published data, actively seek opportunities to create mutual value. It's important to test whether your hypothesis of what you thought was valuable is accurate.

◆ ◆ ◆

Once the negotiation concludes, you enter a critical phase of reflection and learning. This next stage is essential for understanding your negotiation journey and for distilling the insights that will inform your future strategies.

Post-negotiation

Don't cut this phase short as you'll only make future negotiations more challenging if you don't take the learnings available.

Outcome analysis

Take time to reflect on the outcomes in consideration of your initial analysis. How accurate were your predictions? Were there any unexpected developments?

Strategy refinement

What insights have you gained from this negotiation experience that will enhance your strategies and tactics for future negotiations?

Documenting learnings

Make sure to document these key learnings and any new data revealed during the negotiation for future reference (more on this next).

◆ ◆ ◆

Always take the time to do a comprehensive analysis of the negotiation process, reflecting on your strategies and their outcomes. It's this data that will help you extract valuable lessons, refine your approach for future negotiations and make you a more effective negotiator.

Does gathering and analysing data need to be hard?

It's not always easy to find and analyse the *right* data, but there are also a lot of ways we make it hard for ourselves. Sometimes the main challenge isn't so much the data collection or analysis itself, but the way we manage the process of storing and sharing it, either for ourselves, or within our organisation.

How many times have you forgotten a password or couldn't find the information you were looking for? And not because you're collecting it for the first time, but because you've filed it somewhere and now can't remember where.

You may notice a pattern of inefficiency in how data is handled at work and home. Often, at work, teams end up duplicating efforts, not out of choice, but because there's no unified system for data sharing and management. In larger organisations, it's easy for people to be out of the loop and for critical information not to be shared with the right people. At a minimum be clear about your communication plan and test it to determine where the gaps are and what needs to be improved. When we don't consider this it leads to valuable insights and patterns being overlooked because they're not collectively harnessed.

What's more, the issue of data retention becomes critical if there are frequent personnel changes. When colleagues leave, valuable knowledge, often stored in personal inboxes or notes, exits with them. This loss can be a significant setback in building a strong foundation for negotiation strategies.

At home, we don't often apply rigour in setting up simple systems in the way we might need to at work—especially because negotiation isn't top of mind. But imagine if you did keep records of when you last negotiated your salary or an interest rate reduction on your mortgage; for example, what you said, what you were told, what you learned and what you'd do differently? Remember, data analysed becomes information that not only gives us power, but also gives us confidence.

Simplified strategic approaches to managing data

Here are some suggestions for how data can be better captured, stored and shared that apply both at work and home.

Centralise data systems

Keep all your negotiation records in one place. This helps you learn from past experiences to do better in future deals. At home, store all your important receipts for large purchases, contracts (like your rental agreement) or warranty information in a single folder either as a hard copy or on your computer. This makes it easy to refer to when you need to negotiate repairs, returns or renewals. At work, this could be a contract management system that you can use for both storage and retrieval of key contract data.

Knowledge management practices

Make sure you keep notes on what worked and what didn't in your negotiations, and make these notes easy for everyone to find and use. This could be a shared digital document where team members can note down successful strategies or key points from their customer and supplier meetings. At home, this can be done for family members to share the same strategies relevant to the family, such as how and when you last negotiated your utilities or mortgage interest rate. This can help in consistently managing customer and supplier accounts at work or household expenses or family budgets at home.

Use advanced technology

At work, use technology like customer relationship management systems and company-approved AI software to streamline data handling. At home, apps or software can help organise and analyse your negotiation data easily. These tools help you organise, analyse and extract actionable insights more effectively. Imagine if you could point your new team member to all the information that they needed to know about their client—how much would this help them be effective in negotiations? At home, this could be using budget tracking apps or a simple spreadsheet to track your monthly expenses and savings to help you understand your spending patterns and prepare better for financial discussions or decisions.

Build a data-centric negotiation culture

In a work environment, valuable data is lost because people can't see why the data is so valuable and therefore don't record or share them. Developing a culture where data-driven decision-making not only includes objective published data, but also subjective people data would set many businesses apart from their competitors because so many fail to do this well. At home, before making big decisions like buying a car or choosing a holiday destination, gather all relevant information (costs, benefits, reviews) and discuss it with your family. This helps everyone make informed decisions together.

Invest in training and development

Learn more about how to use data in your negotiations. Teach your family or team why it's important and how to do it. Have a family session where you teach each other how to use financial planning tools or discuss articles and tips on effective budgeting and negotiating. This could be about getting better deals on utilities or negotiations for buying/selling items online. At work, recognise that if you're not investing in training, you're investing in people making mistakes and (hopefully) learning from them. There's an expense involved either way, but only one way gives you a clear return on investment—and it's not trial and error.

◆ ◆ ◆

By addressing these areas, at home or at work, you can transform the way data is managed in your day-to-day negotiations. By moving from a fragmented unstructured approach to a streamlined strategic one, you not only make the process more efficient, but also set a strong foundation for you to have more successful negotiation outcomes.

As I've said before, information is not only a source of power, but a source of confidence too. When we back up our decisions with data, be it people or published, we strengthen our position.

Negotiation nuggets:
A — Analyse the data

- *Understand the importance of data*: Data analysis is not just about gaining power, it's about instilling confidence in you. It's crucial for having effective and necessary conversations in negotiations.

- *Perception of data analysis*: Reflect on how you view data analysis, whether it appears daunting or manageable. Be aware your perceptions create your reality. Change your perception to change your reality.

- *There are only two sources of data*:

  - *People data* involves insights from personal interactions and observations, and is crucial for understanding motivations and behaviours.

  - *Published data* includes recorded information, such as reports and statistics, providing an objective basis for positions and strategies.

- *Three lenses for analysing data*: Your perspective, their perspective and an objective perspective. Use these lenses to help you achieve a more rounded and effective preparation process, leading to more successful outcomes.

- *The three stages of negotiation analysis*:

  - *Pre-negotiation* is the time to focus on preparation and planning.

- *During negotiation* pay attention to ongoing data analysis to adapt strategies and identify value creation opportunities in real time.

- *Post-negotiation* is when you should reflect on the negotiation to learn and improve future strategies.

- *Effective data management*: Make it easy for you and your team to store, retrieve and share the valuable data you've gathered and analysed to supercharge your negotiations.

- *Cultivate a data-driven culture*: Help people see the value of the data they have. Develop a culture where data-driven decision-making, using published and people data more effectively, is the norm.

- *Invest in training*: There's an expense involved either way, but only one option gives you a clear return on investment, and it's not trial and error.

Focus five action list: Analyse the data

Action	Activity	Done
Identify key data sources	Focus on two primary sources: people (observations, conversations) and published (reports, market trends).	
Make time for pre-negotiation preparation	Gather and analyse data to identify limits, develop initial offers and understand stakeholder dynamics.	
Adapt during negotiation	Use real-time data to adjust strategies, stay aware of time pressures and seek value creation opportunities.	
Reflect post-negotiation	Analyse outcomes, refine strategies and document learnings for future negotiations.	
Centralise and share data	Implement systems to store and share data effectively, ensuring accessibility and reducing redundancy.	

Chapter 9

L—Understand your leverage

Successfully navigating negotiations often hinges on understanding our advantages, in other words, our leverage. Leverage is our third key to unlocking value, and we're going to look at how you can use it effectively and ethically. I'll also show you how to recognise when someone might be using their leverage against you and how to protect yourself in those situations. The aim is to not only be more skilled at identifying and using your leverage and power, but also to approach negotiations with a mindset that values collaboration, integrity and responsible use of influence.

Defining leverage and power

Think of *leverage* as a specific tool, or advantage, you hold that influences the other party towards an agreement. It could be like having a piece of critical information, facing a deadline that works in your favour, possessing a unique resource or having more options than the other party. The ancient philosopher Archimedes once said, 'Give me a place to stand, and a lever long enough, and I will move the world'. Similarly, in negotiations, if you have something valuable that the other party needs or wants, you hold a powerful position.

Power, on the other hand, is broader and relates to your overall ability to influence outcomes in negotiations. It arises from various sources, such as your position within an organisation, your expertise, your relationships and your access to resources. When others perceive you as capable of affecting their wellbeing through rewards or penalties, your power is enhanced.

It's important that we distinguish between actual and perceived forms of both leverage and power. Actual leverage and power are based on real, tangible, concrete factors—realities that we can directly observe or quantify. Perceived leverage and power, however, depend on others' impressions or beliefs about your capabilities or what you control. Interestingly, perceived power can often be just as effective as actual power in influencing outcomes.

The misconceptions and misuse of leverage

Before we go further, I want to address three common misconceptions about using leverage and power in negotiations.

Misconception 1: You have to overpower the other party

This is not true. Being influential in negotiations doesn't have to involve overpowering or dominating the other party. True power in negotiations can manifest as strength that is used respectfully and collaboratively. This means using power *with* the other party to achieve mutual goals, rather than exerting power *over* them to force your own agenda. For example, if you are a manager negotiating project deadlines with your team, instead of imposing strict deadlines and dictating terms, you might involve them in the decision-making, demonstrating respect for their perspectives and understanding of their workload.

Misconception 2: Power imbalances are inevitable

While it's true that power imbalances can and do exist, in many negotiations they don't have to determine the outcome. Recognising that these imbalances exist is the first step. The next is to consciously aim for equitable solutions that compensate for, or minimise, the impact of these disparities. In labour negotiations, for example, the significant power disparity between management and employees can be neutralised by involving a neutral mediator to ensure all voices are heard and considered.

Misconception 3: Someone always has to lose

Negotiations are not always a zero-sum game, where one party's gain is automatically another's loss. This perspective is not only limiting, but often incorrect. Negotiations frequently present opportunities for mutually beneficial outcomes where all parties can achieve their goals to a greater or lesser extent.

◆ ◆ ◆

Believing that leverage means overpowering others, that power imbalances are fixed and that negotiations must be win-lose, can and will hinder your success. Instead, when we focus on using collaborative strategies, seek creative solutions and aim for sustainable outcomes that benefit all parties, we conduct more effective, equitable and ethical negotiations.

Power vs force

One of the most common challenges I see people navigate, is how to strike a balance between achieving optimal business outcomes and maintaining healthy relationships. The question below, posed by one of my participants, brings to life this challenge in their own words:

> *I struggle not to feel impacted by my, at times, ruthless behaviour. So how do you deal with your own inner voice and, equally, how do you make sure a tough negotiation doesn't go on to souring a working relationship externally?*

This question isn't isolated, it's a fundamental challenge in negotiation. This is because this question isn't just about technique, it's about the ethical and emotional dimensions of negotiation. This challenge requires us to approach negotiations as The Diplomat archetype, which, as I mentioned in Chapter 2, is much harder in practise.

This is where the idea of power versus force comes into play, a concept made popular by David R. Hawkins. He explained the difference between using *power* and using *force* in dealing with people.

According to Hawkins, true *power* is constructive and comes from a place of higher awareness—think of traits such as understanding, peace, love and empathy. This kind of power works because it's natural and genuine, and it influences others positively without needing to force anything, often because, with higher levels of awareness, we see the world more expansively and with greater compassion.

On the flip side, from a lower level of awareness, is *force*. Force is destructive, often driven by negative emotions, such as fear, anger or pride, and involves pushing people to do things. While this might work in the short term, it usually leads to problems like resistance and conflict, which can damage relationships and even break them down over time. Power attracts, supports and serves others, whereas force repels, exploits and is self-serving.

In my own experience with negotiations, I've seen how using power leads to better outcomes. For example, in a negotiation for business unit performance targets, a focus on understanding the team's strengths and the market conditions, including head winds and challenges, while collaboratively setting goals for improvement and offering support, created a positive environment. When we aim for mutual benefits and build trust, everyone involved feels valued and relationships last longer. Conversely, I've also seen the negative effects of using force. In another instance, a leader pushed for more aggressive targets without considering the team's capacity or current challenges. The quick win of locking in the high target also caused quick problems, creating tensions and lasting trust issues. Power fosters a positive, cooperative environment while force often leads to resistance and conflict.

What we also need to be aware of is that force often provokes a counterforce. This is a natural reaction where pushing too hard against someone leads to them pushing back against you. It's like when you compress a spring: the more you push it down, the stronger it springs back once you let go.

When force is used in negotiations, it might seem effective at first because it can compel people to agree or comply out of pressure; however, this kind of compliance is usually temporary. Over time, it builds resentment and resistance. People feel coerced and might look for ways to reverse the situation, balance the scales or even retaliate, which can lead to conflicts and damage relationships in the long run.

Deep down we all know this. My delegate knew this when they asked, 'how do you deal with your own inner voice'. That inner voice was the calm voice of their authentic conscious expression, their ACE, communicating very clearly that their actions were not in alignment with their deeper human values and higher levels of awareness. I'm sure you've felt this too, your inner conflict is often a clear indicator that the path you're taking might not be the natural and best choice for you.

Easy in theory but difficult in practise

Understanding power versus force is straightforward, but applying it in real-world business scenarios is more challenging. Not everyone operates from a higher level of awareness, and as a result, negotiations can often devolve into exertions of force, shifting focus from creating value to simply haggling over prices and costs. I've said this before: it's easy to start off collaboratively and then default to being competitive when the pressure ramps up and the stakes are high.

Let's bring this into perspective with a real-world example. Imagine you're leading a negotiation with a supplier. In this scenario, your company holds more power: you're a key client and the supplier relies heavily on your orders. Traditionally, you might be tempted to use this power to negotiate lower prices more aggressively, prioritising immediate gains, but potentially risking the relationship.

However, you might consider a different approach, one that employs compassionate power instead of force. By recognising your significant influence, you can opt to use it not to press for the lowest price, but to establish a sustainable, mutually beneficial arrangement. For instance, you agree to provide a supplier with security through a long-term contract while requiring them to leverage your company's expertise in lean manufacturing to improve their operations and to pass on any cost savings. This approach ensures that your company receives adequate value, but also allows the supplier to maintain quality and stability. By adopting a more compassionate position, you secure a reliable supply chain and foster a stable, loyal partnership.

This ties back to the inner conflict my delegate faced, highlighting a key insight that, when we operate from a higher level of awareness, we naturally lean towards compassionate power. Moving away from this can harm both ourselves and our relationships.

Some of the most iconic world leaders have demonstrated the use of compassionate power. Nelson Mandela, Mahatma Gandhi and Martin Luther King Jr have all demonstrated that it's not soft or weak to show compassion and understanding. In fact, it was their conscious choice not to exert force that led to sustainable positive agreements like the end of apartheid, India's independence from British rule and equal rights for Black Americans — agreements that benefited all of humanity.

On the opposite end, where leaders have chosen force, one of world's most memorable is Adolf Hitler, who used control, coercion and manipulation, leading to catastrophic consequences and immense human suffering. It's an extreme example, but the same principles apply in the business world too. We've all experienced working with both types of leaders: ones who use power compassionately to inspire positive change and those who command and control, using fear to drive outcomes.

In today's capitalist society, it may sound idealistic, but this philosophical shift is crucial when using leverage in negotiations to create value. Unless we elevate our awareness in business and in life, we risk being trapped in a cycle where leverage is used as a coercive force rather than a tool for mutual benefit and sustainable relationships.

I've lost count of how many times I've seen supermarket shelves stripped of products because either the supplier has stopped supply or the retailer has withdrawn distribution. This is a prime example of lower levels of awareness in action, and the use of coercive force, not power, to create leverage and close a deal.

What's most interesting is that, typically, when both parties believe their power is more equal, we see more use of compassionate power. The use of force is more commonly observed when one party believes they have more power than the other or when they both think that they have more power than each other. That's when the emotional Jokers come out to play and chaos ensues!

Ultimately, the highest form of power builds rather than breaks. It's a compassionate power rooted in integrity, empathy and mutual respect. True power is about aligning our negotiation practises with these higher principles, ensuring that every agreement we make contributes positively to our world.

Case study: $100 million government tender

Tenders are often used by government and private organisations to give suppliers the opportunity to bid for large and complex projects. The process ensures competitiveness across the different suppliers and the selection criteria often cover a multitude of variables, including price, quality and capability, among many others.

In this case, a global people resource supplier was submitting a tender for a five-year contract with a government organisation valued at $100 million. While the process itself creates competition between suppliers, encouraging them to put their best foot forward, what was fascinating in this situation was how this government organisation leveraged force rather than compassionate power.

First, the deadline was only 45 days from the announcement of the tender, yet the consideration period from the deadline to the award was four months. The tender brief included stringent requirements, such as any incomplete data in the tender submissions (meaning representatives may need to ask follow-up questions) resulting in the bid being rejected outright.

In addition, there was no opportunity for information gathering and any questions had to be submitted in writing and were answered by unidentifiable contract representatives. Once the tenders were submitted, the supplier found out that several of their competitors were being asked clarifying questions post the deadline, in contravention of the rules. Six weeks after the award deadline, the supplier was notified that they were unsuccessful, without receiving the opportunity to present their proposal in person.

The fact that this was a five-year partnership should have indicated that this needed to be a collaborative process between the government organisation and the respective suppliers. They should have had the opportunity to ask and

(continued)

receive questions and to understand who the suppliers were and how they could work together effectively.

By using force (rigid timelines, inflexible rules, a lack of communication and transparency), the government organisation created an environment of mistrust and frustration. In contrast, if they had used power differently (approaching the process with empathy, openness and a genuine interest in collaboration), they could have fostered a more positive and productive relationship with the suppliers, one that was aligned on value and built on trust, delivering significantly more value.

The poor planning of the government organisation who issued the tender led to them being forced to maintain their existing supplier for a further twelve months. The inefficiency in the process meant they didn't have enough time for the incoming supplier to be resourced and begin implementing their solution before the renewal period for the existing supplier, souring the relationships with the other bidders.

What gives you power?

To be effective in negotiations, it's important to recognise the sources of power at our disposal. There are several different types of power you can leverage during negotiations. Remember, 'with great power comes great responsibility'. Our approach, whether we use power or force, reflects our core values and ethics, especially when tested in practical scenarios.

The power of options (next best options or NBOs)

- *Power* looks like you having multiple options, enhancing your flexibility and reducing pressure to agree to less favourable terms. This freedom allows you to look for and propose solutions that benefit all parties involved.

- *Force* looks like you having many options and using these alternatives as leverage to press for one-sided gains, exploiting the other party's lack of choices.

The power of time

- *Power* looks like you aren't under tight time constraints, but the other party is, and you use this advantage to facilitate a thoughtful, deliberate negotiation process that considers all angles and perspectives.

- *Force* looks like you misusing this time constraint as an advantage to pressure the other party into making hasty decisions as deadlines loom, often leading to unfavourable terms for them.

The power of information

- *Power* looks like gaining exclusive insights to shift the dynamics of a negotiation. Using this information transparently to build trust and cooperation, encouraging open dialogue about your concerns and goals.

- *Force* looks like choosing to use this information strategically to exploit the other party's vulnerabilities for competitive gain.

The power of size and scale

- *Power* looks like leveraging your extensive resources to support and lead industry-wide initiatives that promote sustainability and innovation; contributing to elevating standards across the sector, benefiting all players and fostering a healthier industry environment.

- *Force* looks like using your resources to overwhelm smaller competitors by escalating operations, or using financial strength to prolong negotiations, effectively wearing down the other party to push through favourable terms.

The power of process

- *Power* looks like implementing a transparent and structured negotiation process that ensures that all parties are treated fairly, contributing to a more equitable outcome.

- *Force* looks like the process disproportionately favours one side, leading to resentment and a breakdown of trust.

The power of environment

- *Power* looks like creating a conducive negotiation environment that promotes comfort and equality to enhance openness and parity among all participants.

- *Force* looks like deliberately configuring the setting to disadvantage others to provide an undue psychological edge.

The power of legitimacy

- *Power* looks like significant organisational changes, such as leadership transitions or mergers, providing a legitimate platform for renegotiating terms to align with the goals and values of all stakeholders.

- *Force* looks like these occasions being misused to aggressively advance personal agendas, overlooking the broader interests of other stakeholders.

The power of deadlock

- *Power* looks like approaching deadlock as a chance for collaborative problem-solving, leading to innovative solutions that accommodate all parties.

- *Force* looks like exploiting a deadlock to exhaust the other party's resources and coerce them into unfavourable agreements.

The power of market dominance

- *Power* looks like leveraging your significant market share responsibly to help foster a sustainable industry environment that supports all players, including smaller competitors.

- *Force* looks like imposing unfair conditions that exploit smaller competitors or manipulating market prices to hinder new entrants.

These examples illustrate how the same source of power can be used positively or negatively, depending on the approach. What's important to state here is that the choice of collaborating and sharing information is never made naively. Compassionate power is always used wisely with the appropriate risk assessment of the other party's will and skill level. In every circumstance, you can choose power over force and still be in a position where you protect yourself and your business from being exploited.

Employing compassionate power in negotiations is about creating beneficial outcomes for all parties involved. But this brings us to another important aspect of negotiations: the concept of fairness. Often, our understanding of fairness is deeply ingrained, yet, as we'll see, it can be a misleading guide in negotiations.

Fairness is a fallacy

From a very young age, we're taught about the value of fairness. Growing up, my mum's value for fairness ensured that my sister and I always had an equal amount of money spent on us for our birthdays, whether it was giving us money, a helping hand for a home deposit or a gift. My mum made sure neither of us was benefiting more than the other. The sense of fairness she instilled in me was that it equalled 50:50.

The role fairness played in my life continued into adulthood and into relationships where I financially contributed 50:50. Fairness meant equal, right? Wrong. I learned that some of my friends and colleagues had different perspectives on what was fair. They approached finances differently in their relationships. Some would contribute based on their percentage of the combined earnings, and others would pool everything together in one family account and spend without concern for how much each person contributed—it was 'family money', and that was fair.

What it taught me about fairness was that it is subjective, and that people have very different ideas of what is fair. As a simple example, what if I give you an orange and tell you to share it fairly with me? Would you cut it in half and share it? Would that be fair? What if I only needed the zest and you were interested in the juice? Would that be a good deal? It leaves both of us not getting what we want—fairness isn't the answer to getting the best outcome.

The challenge with fairness is that, even if at a human level we all understand and acknowledge life isn't fair, our need for fairness can be as strong as our need to be valued. So, in negotiations, the agreements we seek to make must give the perception of being fair in the eyes of the other party or else they won't want to agree to the deal.

Imagine you bought a lottery ticket and ended up winning $5 million. The only condition attached to you being able to keep it is that you share it with a friend. The rules of the lottery are clear and visible to everyone, so your friend is aware of the rules too. You have been asked to select the percentage you will offer your friend. You get one offer only, and they must either accept your offer or reject it. If they reject the offer, neither party gets to keep anything. If they accept, you both walk away with money. What would you offer?

I ask participants to role-play a similar scenario in my workshops, and the outcomes I get are usually very different across each of the pairings. Some get deals, others don't. Applying logic would say we should always accept the deal because we both walk away with money that we didn't have before. But negotiations aren't logical; they are emotional decisions that we justify with logic. Fairness, we must remember, is very subjective. So even if you think you're being fair, the other party may reject the deal because they didn't feel the same way.

In seeking to be fair, at best, you walk away with 50 per cent of the available value and, at worst, you walk away with significantly less. If you remember only one thing from this book, remember this: fairness is a fallacy. Your objective isn't to be fair but to maximise the exchange of value by discovering each party's needs and positioning value appropriately.

How we influence

To be effective in negotiations we need to be able to influence others. Influence is generally seen as a subtler form of power. It involves shaping how people think and feel, leading them to act in a certain way more voluntarily. Influence uses leverage, persuasion, charisma and other non-coercive methods to sway our decisions and behaviours. It's subtler because it works by altering our internal motivations and attitudes. While it doesn't force us to act against our will, it does work to align our will with the influencer's goals.

In his book *Influence: The Psychology of Persuasion*, social scientist Dr Robert Cialdini identified seven core principles of influence:

- *Reciprocity:* We feel an obligation to give back when we receive something.

- *Scarcity:* We want more of something that is limited.

- *Authority:* We follow those with expertise or status.

- *Consistency:* We want to be in alignment with our previous statements/actions.

- *Liking:* We say 'yes' more to the people we like.

- *Social proof:* We use the influence of what others are doing; for example, reading testimonials to help make a decision.

- *Unity:* We build connection over a shared sense of identity.

These principles are often used as leverage and forms of psychological power, where a person uses their behaviour to influence ours without us even realising. There are two reasons why it is important to think about this: first, to enhance your influencing and persuasion skills through the ethical use of these principles, and second, to enable you to protect yourself from being manipulated, or unduly influenced, by others who are being less than ethical.

I've adapted Cialdini's work and plotted his seven principles against two axes (see figure 9.1, overleaf):

- *Value driver:* The vertical axis is used to determine whether intrinsic (internal) or extrinsic (external) factors are the primary drivers of value for each principle. This axis illustrates the underlying motivation behind each principle's effectiveness; essentially, it explains why the principle works. Intrinsic drivers relate to internal values and personal motivation, while extrinsic drivers involve external social rewards and recognition.

- *Method of influence:* The horizontal axis is used to assess whether the influence exerted by each principle is rational or emotional. This helps to clarify how the principle is typically applied in practise. A rational method of influence appeals to logical reasoning, evidence and cognitive processes. An emotional method of influence, on the other hand, appeals to feelings, emotions and affective responses.

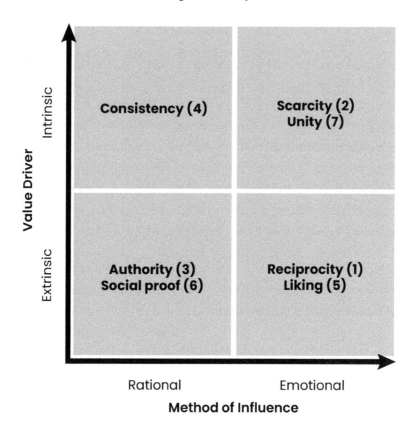

Figure 9.1 Cialdini's seven principles

Source: Adapted from *Influence: The Psychology of Persuasion by Dr Robert Cialdini.*

1. Extrinsic value driver and rational method of influence

The principles positioned in the lower left quadrant of figure 9.1 employ a rational approach to influencing others. Here, the value is derived from external factors; for example, social etiquette, professional recognition, and professional or social reputation. The methods used to exert influence appeal to our logic brain, reason and evidence.

Authority

This principle follows the premise that we have a deeply ingrained obedience to authority figures, something we're taught to comply with from a young age, whether it be teachers, parents or uniformed police officers. This means that we instinctively give trust to people who have authority and are more inclined to listen to them and follow their guidance. Authority itself appeals to logical reasoning. Our authority, whether it comes through position, expertise or knowledge, must be clearly signalled to the other party before we can seek to influence them.

In negotiation, being a credible authority with deep subject matter expertise in your market gives you leverage, in that it adds weight to your recommendations and proposals. Authority also carries greater weight if someone else speaks to your credibility rather than you doing so yourself. From a power perspective, authority gives you power in your seniority and status. You can have power directly within an organisation, or even as a third party, through being a credible authority.

Social proof

Imagine you're walking down a street looking for something to eat, and you pass two restaurants you've not been to before. One is busy and has people lining up outside waiting to be seated, and the other has a handful of people inside with lots of empty tables. In the absence of certainty in knowing which to choose, we are more likely to follow the crowd based on the principle of social proof. The assumption we make is that if others are choosing it, it must be the right choice. It relies on us using external and visible measures of value (bums on seats) to reduce our perceived risk in making the wrong choice.

In negotiation, we can use social proof as a logic-based lever to demonstrate the value others have received from implementing our product or service. Social proof can also be a form of power through demonstrated conformity; for example, if the widespread adoption of your methods has set a new standard for the industry, the conformity demonstrates your legitimacy.

2. Intrinsic value driver and rational method of influence

This upper left quadrant represents the principles of influence that appeal to logic and reasoning, but speak to our deeper internal motivations, such as core values and psychological needs—things that are personal to us.

Consistency

This principle of influence is used with the knowledge that we have a logical desire to be seen as consistent with our self-image, and with things we've previously done or said. When we make commitments to others publicly, we face personal and interpersonal pressure to act in alignment with those commitments. Consistency is highly valued and so it's difficult to act against the self-image we have of ourselves and what we want others to see.

In negotiations, a consistent track record for following through on your commitments gives you power through credibility and makes it logically more likely that others will want to deal with you when people know what they can expect. As a lever, you could use the consistency principle to get people to make small commitments initially, opening them up to the possibility of making larger commitments later as part of their commitment to working together.

3. Intrinsic value driver and emotional method of influence

This upper right quadrant represents the principles of influence that appeal to our feelings and emotions driven by deeper internal motivations, such as core values, beliefs and self-identity.

Scarcity

This principle recognises that, as humans, we tend to assign greater value to things that are scarce and we fear missing out on. The FOMO drives a sense of urgency to make a decision and take action that we may not otherwise take if the availability or access of this deal was not limited in some way.

Even with the knowledge of this principle, I've seen how powerful it is in driving action. It's because scarcity can trigger our survival instinct, which makes it much harder to walk away if we feel that we are going to lose something.

In negotiations, scarcity is a powerful lever to encourage decision-making, especially if urgency is created with a limited-time offer and the other party feels they need to act to secure it. As scarcity directly appeals to an internal value driver, it could also shift the balance of power in your favour if the other party feels they have more to lose by not accepting.

If you're the only one who can provide what the other party needs, the scarcity of alternative options will mean you have greater influence. But beware of abusing your position, especially as this scenario doesn't last long as people seek to cover single points of risk and will look for alternatives so that they are not restricted to one choice.

Unity

This principle taps into our human need for belonging. We see it most commonly with sports fans who often refer to the teams they support as 'my' team and discuss how the team played using language that unites them, such as '*we* had such a tough game this weekend'.

In negotiations that require long-term relationship building, unity builds a shared sense of identity to form a stronger emotional bond. As a lever, discussing shared goals and values can create a sense of partnership and belonging.

4. Extrinsic value driver and emotional method of influence

The principles of influence in the lower right quadrant represent those principles that appeal to feelings and emotions more than logic. The value driver is external, such as social rewards, recognition and connection.

Reciprocity

Have you ever noticed how, when a friend buys you a present for your birthday, you feel an automatic sense of obligation to do the same for them, even if you're not that close and weren't expecting them to buy you a present in the first place? Or how about when someone unexpectedly buys you a coffee at work and you feel that you need to buy them a coffee next time round?

In negotiations, when we understand that, as humans, we all feel a sense of social obligation to give something back (maintain social balance), the law of reciprocity can be a key lever for gaining agreement. If we give something of value to someone first, they are more likely to want to give us something in return. When negotiations get tricky and parties get entrenched in their positions, a powerful way to encourage movement is to make the first concession, this encourages the other party to make a move in return, because reciprocity leverages feelings of obligation and gratitude.

Over time, this also becomes a form of power and, as Adam Grant shares in his book *Give and Take*, it's the givers that win in the long run. When you develop a reputation for being someone who has a history of helping others, you create the opportunity for people to return the favour for you when you need it most.

Liking

This principle leverages positive feelings and social bonds and recognises that we are more likely to say 'yes' to people we like than those we don't. We create positive association with people who pay us compliments, who work with us towards achieving mutual goals and those we feel are like us.

In negotiations, the liking principle can be used as a positive lever through investing time in building rapport and connections to find common interests. Those taking a more direct and obvious approach to rapport building can still influence short-term interactions, but often only at a surface level of connection—we can all tell when someone is going through the motions at a transactional level. For greater depth in relationships, emotional influence is more subtle, nuanced and takes time to nurture.

As a form of power, being likeable means people enjoy and look forward to working with you, which gives you an advantage over other parties.

In understanding these principles, we can be more aware of when they are being used on us and protect ourselves from easily being manipulated. When we can see the persuasion tactics being used, it enables us to take a more critical and thoughtful perspective before making any agreements, and allows our decision-making to be more informed by acknowledging where we may be unduly influenced by psychology drivers outside the merits of the case. It also helps us recognise our own influence and understand how our words and actions can influence others, often subconsciously.

If we don't understand leverage, power and influence, our ability to secure successful outcomes in negotiations will be significantly compromised. Knowing that perceived power and leverage is just as effective as actual power and leverage helps us recognise that we can always influence better outcomes, even when we think we are operating from a place of weakness.

Negotiation nuggets:
L — Understand your leverage

- *Understand your leverage*: It's crucial for you to recognise what leverage you possess in any negotiation. This knowledge is a game changer, providing you with a strategic advantage to steer conversations toward favourable outcomes.

- *The power-leverage connection*: Distinguish between your leverage and your overall power in a negotiation. Understanding the interplay between these two can greatly enhance your effectiveness and influence in achieving your goals.

- *Rethink leverage misconceptions*: Let go of the idea that leverage means overpowering others or that a power imbalance dictates outcomes. Negotiation isn't about winners and losers; it's about finding mutually beneficial solutions.

- *The ethical use of power*: Learn to approach negotiations with compassionate power rather than force. This approach helps achieve your objectives and builds lasting, positive relationships.

- *Apply power and leverage in real scenarios*: Practise using your leverage in ways that are ethical and productive. By doing so, you create a balance between getting what you want and maintaining healthy business relationships.

- *Fairness is subjective*: Understand that fairness in negotiations is often a matter of perception. Strive for agreements that feel equitable to all parties involved, rather than sticking rigidly to a 50:50 division.

- *The art of influence*: Grasp the principles of influence outlined by Dr Robert Cialdini and apply them judiciously. Your ability to influence effectively can make or break a negotiation.

- *Dealing with various power dynamics*: Be prepared for negotiations where power dynamics vary. Whether you perceive yourself as more or less powerful, your understanding of these dynamics can guide you to negotiate more effectively.

Focus five action list: Understand your leverage

Action	Activity	Done
Identify and assess leverage	List your unique advantages, such as critical resources, exclusive information or multiple options. Use this list to understand how these can strengthen your negotiation position.	
Distinguish between power and force	Use power ethically. Apply leverage in a way that fosters collaboration and mutual benefit, avoiding coercive tactics that could harm relationships.	
Understand power dynamics	Map out both the actual and perceived power between parties. Evaluate the balance of power, including how your leverage might be perceived by the other party.	
Employ ethical influence	Use principles of influence. Leverage Cialdini's principles, including reciprocity, authority and social proof to ethically persuade and influence negotiation outcomes.	
Prepare for power imbalances	Identify power disparities and plan specific approaches to neutralise them, where possible. Use strategies like a neutral location and finding common ground to balance power dynamics effectively.	

Chapter 10

U — Embrace feeling uncomfortable

The fourth key to the Value Model is to *embrace feeling uncomfortable*. Our biggest opportunities for growth often emerge from what makes us uncomfortable. We all face moments that challenge us, pushing us out of our comfort zones. Negotiation, at its core, is an exercise in stepping into the unknown, into situations that might not always feel comfortable. Yet, it's precisely in these moments that we find our greatest potential for growth and contribution.

The need for comfort in negotiations can lead us down paths that are less fruitful than those that challenge us. Comfort can lead to accepting the first offer to avoid discomfort like The Accommodator archetype, not countering a proposal for the ease of agreement or folding quickly under pressure. When we prioritise comfort, we might miss

utilising time or the surrounding circumstances effectively in the negotiation, focusing too much on avoiding the discomfort that is a natural part of the process.

Stepping out of your comfort zone in negotiations is about understanding the power of your emotions in these interactions and steering clear of choices that lessen the value you exchange. Comfort often leads to complacency, and in high-stakes negotiation, whether professionally or personally, complacency is the last thing you can afford.

The cost of staying in your comfort zone

Even as a negotiation specialist, there are moments I wish I could rewind and do over. I had arranged to view a new house and, on arrival, the agent told me that she'd had a buyer come through during the week and put down a deposit with an unconditional offer. My heart sank. I didn't understand why she'd continued holding the open house when it was no longer available. She saw the look on my face and then told me she had another house two doors down, built to the same spec, that wasn't yet advertised, but she'd be happy to show us. It was the last house available on the street in an area we wanted to live, so we negotiated an offer $50 000 less than the asking price, with finance conditions and a longer settlement date, which was accepted. There was one vital question I'd failed to ask during the negotiation though: How much had the other property been sold for? It wasn't a question I had forgotten to ask; it was a question I felt *uncomfortable* asking. I was afraid that the person may have offered a higher price, and I didn't want to be anchored to it. In subsequent months, when the house price was published, I found out the house two doors up sold for the same price I had negotiated.

While it was a relief, my heart also sank as it confirmed my suspicion that by not gathering all the information available, I had missed the opportunity to potentially negotiate a better deal. We've all hesitated at times and what I've learned is best summed up by Lewis Carroll, 'In the end...We only regret the chances we didn't take, the relationships we were afraid to have, and the decisions we waited too long to make.'

I still feel discomfort in my body when it comes to negotiating. I also know the more I continue my practise, the more refined my methods become, but still my body feels the discomfort. What I've shared with all my participants training to improve their negotiations skills is that negotiating is *supposed* to feel uncomfortable, so feeling this way is quite normal. If we're negotiating effectively, it will never feel comfortable. Yet, the inclination to feel comfortable and relaxed is what most of us naturally yearn for in negotiations.

A common dilemma in negotiations is the desire to avoid difficult questions due to discomfort. Here are some steps to ensure you don't fall into this trap.

- *Prepare your questions:* Before entering any negotiation, prepare a list of essential questions. Include even those that make you uncomfortable — they are often the most crucial.

- *Practise discomfort:* Role-play negotiations with a friend or colleague, focusing on asking those tough questions. This practise can desensitise you to the discomfort and make you more confident in real situations. I once worked in a business where my CEO and group CFO would spend hours over several weeks role-playing their budget presentation to the board for sign off.

- *Recognise the value of information:* Understand that every piece of information can be leveraged in a negotiation.

The more you know, the better positioned you are to make beneficial decisions. As Richard Shell suggests, determine in advance what information you will openly *give* the other party, what information you need to *get,* and what information you will need to *guard* or keep confidential.

- *Shift your mindset:* Instead of viewing tough questions as a source of discomfort, consider them opportunities to gain a more favourable outcome. Changing your perspective can change your approach. This is exactly the mindset my CEO and group CFO had when preparing their responses to potential questions from the board. Because of their efforts, they were rarely asked for a budget number higher than their original submission.

Understanding and managing our emotions and discomfort during negotiations is a vital part of the process. But it's not just about what we feel; it's also about how we express those feelings through our words. Our language choices play a crucial role in the dynamics and outcomes of our negotiations.

Watch your language

How many times have you heard 'watch your language'? Perhaps it's something you say to your children? Typically, it's because they've used language that's inappropriate, offensive or not suitable given their context or the audience. The prompt 'watch your language' is essentially a reminder for us to speak more considerately or appropriately.

In a negotiation, this prompt couldn't be more accurate. As I've mentioned, negotiations are meant to be uncomfortable, but what happens is that our bodies 'leak' our discomfort through the words we say and our body language. What I loved about being inducted into the world of negotiation early in my career was that it opened my eyes and ears to the ways in which we leak value. While it was horrifying to learn how much value I was giving away by being careless with my words, the upside of this is that I started to hear and see people differently. It's like the superpower I'd wished for as an awkward teenager — 'I wish I knew what they were thinking', had in some way become available to me.

The words we choose are of significant importance in negotiations because they can impact our position and the value we exchange. I can always tell the difference between an amateur negotiator with no training versus someone who has been trained, because they don't watch their language in the same way. You've probably heard the saying, 'Loose lips sink ships', meaning beware of unguarded talk. This idiom originated in World War II campaigns created by the War Advertising Council to prevent defence personnel and citizens undermining the war effort through careless talk.

In the context of negotiation, we often resort to using looser language when we feel uncomfortable; we also use more words to ease our discomfort. It's our body's way of soothing our stress. To prevent yourself from undermining your negotiation efforts, I want you to consciously remember this: *Loose language leaks value.*

You might be surprised how some common turns of phrase can be perceived by a counterpart. Next time you go to use one of these phrases, consider what value you may be leaking.

- *Ideally, I would like to or my preference would be:* These phrases suggests that your position is more of a preference than a firm requirement.

- *I'm hoping/aiming for around or I can probably do:* The use of *hoping, aiming, probably* and *around* suggest you are not fixed on a specific number or requirement.

- *I could possibly consider or I'm looking for something in the range of:* These phrases imply room for movement rather a specific figure.

- *I'm looking for:* This suggests your current position is one of searching for opportunity rather than a clear firm need.

- *Our goal is to get close to or my target is:* This shows that you're aiming for a figure but are open to variations around it.

- *My opening offer is:* Saying this indicates you have other offers and are not expecting this initial one to be accepted.

Because this language suggests a lack of firmness in your position, it tells us that you're open to movement or compromise. Any skilled negotiator would use this information to steer the negotiation, leveraging your flexibility to create an advantage. In collaborative, high trust negotiation environments, these leaks of information regarding your position may not harm you as much as they would in a more competitive situation, but either way, because you're giving up your leverage and putting it in the hands of another party, it's likely to reduce the value you exchange.

Instead, I encourage you to use tighter, more assertive language, such as the phrases in table 10.1. Say *I need, I can accept* or *If you can do this, then I can do that.* This approach signals that you're firm, precise and concise in communicating your needs, and it conveys that you are in your power. This makes it much harder for the other party to take advantage of any internal discomfort you may feel.

Table 10.1 closing language leaks

Loose language	A firmer alternative
Ideally, I would like to …	My requirement is … .
I'm hoping/aiming for around …	I'm prepared to commit to … .
I could possibly consider …	I will accept … .
I'm looking for …	I specifically need … .
I can probably do …	I will do … .
Our goal is to get close to …	We must achieve … .
My preference would be …	My condition is … .
My target is …	My position is … .
I'm looking for something in the range of …	I need it to be … .
My opening offer is …	My offer/price is … .

Leaking value through loose language can occur with small things, like leakages of our time when we say, 'I'll see what I can do', instead of saying, 'I don't have capacity to meet that request this week'. Whether it's communicating boundaries or negotiating a high-value deal, the language we use is incredibly important.

The use of tight language, on the other hand, is firm and concise, and indicates a stronger, unmoving stance. This doesn't mean that you aren't moveable, but it does mean the emphasis is put on the other party to find that out by negotiating the value they want to exchange in return. Embrace your discomfort and tighten your words, remembering that power in negotiation often lies in not just what you say, but how you say it.

Case study: Maya's audiobook deal

When Maya came to me with an offer she'd received for the audio rights to her book, she didn't know how to craft a response that would help her secure more. The company was based internationally, and the offer was made over email, which wasn't ideal as she didn't have an existing relationship with the sender. She'd been offered a lump sum that would be payable 50 per cent on signing and 50 per cent on publication, as well as any royalties for the different distribution methods. She wanted a 25 per cent increase on the offer and was going to make a request by email to see what was possible.

When she talked me through what she was planning to say, all I could hear was a long-winded justification before saying she wanted 25 per cent more. It wasn't a response positioned from a place of strength, it seemed more like a plea. I talked her through what she should consider in her use of language, the amount she was proposing, how best to position herself and prime her counterpart as well as how she could use the different levers that were available to be negotiated. Following our conversation I asked her to draft the email. Here is her first attempt:

Hi X,

Thank you for this proposal.

As I was already underway with the recording of an audiobook with a contractor in order to self-publish, I'd be willing to consider it at a price of [+75 per cent of original offer] (50 per cent on signing, 25 per cent on recording, 25 per cent on publication).

I look forward to discussing this further with you.

Maya

What worked well was that she focused on sharing what she would be willing to consider rather than what she wouldn't, which would keep the conversation moving towards an outcome. Her counter proposal was a 75 per cent increase on the original offer enabling room for negotiation and the amended breakdown in the payment schedule meant she would get more of the cash sooner.

What was missing was priming ahead of her counter proposal. She needed to influence the perception of her value before making her proposal to avoid appearing greedy or unreasonable. We looked at the different ways we could increase her value in their eyes through positioning, and considered how we could make getting a deal signed attractive for them based on what they valued, which would be audience reach and sales, not just what Maya valued. We also needed to create some urgency for them to respond so that a decision could be made on which direction she was going to take. Here's the rewrite:

Hi X,

Appreciate you reaching out. It's been a busy start to the year, with an increasing number of local and international speaking requests making managing my calendar across the different time zones a little challenging!

(continued)

Thanks for your offer. It's good to see the detail you've provided, and that Company X has the adequate platform to support a strong reach for my audiobook.

Provided that you can agree to an advance of [+75 per cent of original offer] (50 per cent on signature, 25 per cent on recording, 25 per cent on publication), I would be willing to accept the remainder of your terms detailed below and sign up with Company X.

I am, however, in discussion with another potential partner so would need confirmation of this agreement within the next 10 days.

Look forward to hearing from you.

Maya

After sending this email, Maya received a revised offer within 24 hours of +50 per cent of the original offer and 100 per cent payment upfront with no reduction on royalties. Both parties got what they wanted and there was satisfaction in getting to a deal. Maya secured double the amount she would have settled for with much more favourable payment terms. While email wasn't the recommended approach, it did help Maya to make the ask that she wouldn't have otherwise made.

Stop filling the gap

How many times have you found yourself continuing to speak after making a proposal, despite knowing you should have stopped? Perhaps you've filled gaps with unnecessary filler words like 'um', 'uh', 'you know', and 'like'. This often occurs when we're caught in the act of thinking and speaking at the same time, using these fillers either to construct our thoughts or because we're uneasy with silence.

Our inclination to over-talk when uncomfortable is another way our bodies react to stress. It's a response that requires intentional practise to manage. A critical, but often overlooked tool in managing this, is silence. It's incredibly powerful in negotiations and can strengthen your position in unexpected ways. Adam Grant describes this perfectly:

In negotiation, silence is golden. It's not a display of strength that intimidates the other person into giving up value. It's an occasion for reflection that allows you to create value. Pauses make it possible to identify ways to expand the pie, leading to win-win solutions.

Understanding the true power of silence—creating space for thought and reflection rather than intimidation—is vital. The real challenge arises when stress hinders our clarity of thought, pushing silence to the back of our minds. To counteract this, the first step is calming our nervous system, and a great method for this, is box breathing. Visualise drawing a box with each breath cycle: inhale for four counts, hold for four, exhale for four, then hold again for four (see figure 10.1, overleaf). This technique not only soothes the nervous system, but also enhances your capacity to think clearly and make intentional choices in what you say and do.

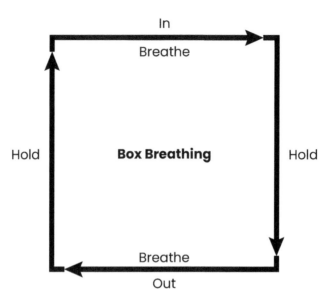

Figure 10.1 box breathing

After presenting your proposal, resist the urge to immediately fill the silence. Allowing a pause gives the other person time to consider your offer and prevents you from diluting your position through nervous chatter. Similarly, when you pose a question, let it linger. Give the other person a moment to respond and use that time to gauge their tone and flexibility. When it's your turn to reply, a brief pause helps you gather your thoughts and avoid unnecessary fillers.

When we pay attention to the other person's reactions in these moments of silence, it can reveal a lot about what's going through their head. Remember, controlling the narrative isn't just about the words you choose; it's about knowing when to let the silence speak for you. We often feel the need to fill every silence, especially under stress, but embracing these quiet moments can be a real game changer in negotiations.

Watch your body language

It's not just about the words we say or how we say them, it's what our body is doing while we're saying them that can also reveal a lot. When we're negotiating, it's natural to feel stressed. This stress can manifest in several physical ways: your heart beats faster, your breathing becomes shallow and your eyes might start darting around. It's common to find maintaining eye contact difficult, and you might catch yourself speaking faster than usual. All these are signs that we're uncomfortable, and they're signals we're unintentionally sending to the other person.

You might notice your face getting flushed or find yourself touching your nose more often than usual. These are typical reactions to the discomfort we feel in a negotiation setting. What's important is recognising these as natural responses to stress and learning to manage them. Management begins with awareness of our behaviour patterns. Do you scratch your head, fidget with your hands or touch your neck when making a proposal? Observe and understand these 'tells', both in yourself and others. When you're aware of your own body language, you can better manage the message you're sending out. The goal here is to convey confidence and control through your body language, not just your words.

I've always been fascinated by police crime dramas, and I remember being absolutely hooked by the television series *Lie to Me* when it first aired in 2009. It featured actor Tim Roth playing character Cal Lightman, a former police officer and a leading deception expert who studied facial and involuntary body language to discover if someone was lying. It was a series based on the scientific discoveries of American psychologist and professor Dr Paul Ekman, who discovered micro expressions, which are brief, involuntary facial expressions.

You don't need to watch this series to learn more about body language because you're likely to already be an expert. We watch and observe people all the time. We've all watched reality TV shows and, even if you weren't aware you were doing it, analysed the body language of the participants, making interpretations about what their body language means. We notice the involuntary micro expressions that are captured on camera and form our own meanings on what the participant is thinking or feeling.

When we're negotiating for agreement, especially when we're seeking value beyond what we've previously accessed or if we're out of our comfort zone, our body language leaks out in the same way our words leak out. In my workshops, I show my participants what happens when they're stressed or under pressure by recording them and playing it back frame by frame. It's confronting, but it's one of the best ways for them to see, in a safe environment, what their body language is saying as often they have no awareness of what they're doing under pressure.

As Swiss psychologist Carl Jung once said, 'until you make the unconscious conscious, it will direct your life and you will call it fate'. Making our own behaviours conscious isn't easy, but we can begin to raise our awareness by first observing others more carefully and trying to make sense of what we see.

Here are five ways you can start to make the unconscious conscious.

1. Watch for self-soothing gestures

When we're stressed or uncomfortable, we naturally seek to soothe ourselves. This self-soothing behaviour can look like face touching, fidgeting or other pacifying behaviours. Nearly twenty years on from my very first training workshop as a participant, I still remember how my colleague Mike used to lean back in his chair and raise his hand up to touch the back of his neck. He only did this when he was about to make a proposal and it showed me his 'tell' for when he was uncomfortable.

'What the human body does—and it does it exquisitely—is display psychological discomfort in real time', says Joe Navarro, a former FBI counter-intelligence officer and author of *What EveryBODY Is Saying*. 'King Charles—he's always playing with his cufflinks. This is how he deals with social anxiety. Prince Harry—he's always buttoning the button that's already buttoned—another comforting behaviour.' Ask a close friend or family member if they can help you identify how you soothe yourself when you're uncomfortable.

2. Look for mismatches between words and gestures

Given that our bodies give away our psychological discomfort in real time, it's highly likely that, even if we have tightened up the words we use verbally, our unspoken language might still be saying something else. For this reason, it's important to listen to the words the other party is saying and reference them with their accompanying body language—this can better help you spot their discomfort, uncertainty and, potentially, their dishonesty. For example, your colleague might tell you they are 'completely on board' with your proposal of working late to meet a project deadline, but you notice they are shifting in their seat and looking away towards their phone as they say this. These signs could indicate their hesitance or reservation about your proposal, suggesting a further discussion might be needed to address their underlying concerns.

3. Don't rely solely on obvious gestures

According to the 7-38-55 rule, developed by psychology professor Albert Mehrabian, 93 per cent of meaning is communicated without words. That means, 7 per cent of meaning is communicated through the words we use, 38 per cent of meaning is communicated in our tone of voice, and 55 per cent is communicated in our body language. As such, the meaning of our feelings is mostly communicated in our reactions and our tone rather than our words.

How many times has someone influenced your behaviour just by the way they've looked at you or the sound they've made in response to what you've said? I vividly remember in one of my workshops how one of my participants responded to an initial proposal made by another party. He responded with his eyes wide open, his head pulling back and in a raised and surprised tone he uttered one word, 'Wow'. The impact it had on the other party was incredible, he looked confused, apologised, started to re-check his notes and found himself losing his composure, quickly unravelling his strong proposal.

In negotiations, be cautious of overt displays of emotion or dramatic gestures, as these could be performed for effect and could mislead you. A flinch when receiving a proposal is one of the easiest ways we can influence and be influenced.

4. Learn to receive, not transmit

I can't tell you how often I see people with their head down writing notes at crucial moments when the other party is giving them the most telling information about what they mean through their body language. You can't interpret the unspoken language if you've essentially put your blindfold on. While writing effective notes is absolutely necessary, we have to make sure we do so at non-critical moments of communication. There are other ways to manage this too, such as asking a team member to take notes on your behalf, using a note-taker on an online video call or simply requesting permission to record the meeting so that you can be fully present.

5. Notice emotional leakage

Emotional leakage is when someone's true emotions momentarily surface, which are usually in contrast to what they're expressing consciously. It's a fleeting micro expression that could be telling. This could be an initial flash of anger, immediately replaced by a smile, which could indicate a hidden disagreement or feeling of hostility. It could also be an indication of surprise with the lift of their eyebrows before neutralising their facial expression.

You may also have experienced unintentional laughter and smiling at inappropriate times, which can be sign of nervousness or discomfort. When my father died in car accident in 2006, I still remember how horrified I was that, when I was breaking the news to my mum, I could feel a smile breaking on my face. It was a very confronting nervous reaction, made worse as I remember her being confused by my facial expression and asking me if I was serious, which sadly I was. For a long time, I didn't understand why I was smiling until I began to understand human behaviour better.

What I've learned about body language over the years is that specific gestures don't always have specific meanings. What we communicate through our body language can be ambiguous and affected by multiple factors, such as mood, comfort or environment. Our face also doesn't always express our true feelings, as adults we often mask our emotions to maintain social and professional harmony. Strong emotions can leak through in micro expressions that are often fleeting and difficult to catch.

The key thing to remember is that body language is more about understanding emotional intent than what someone is consciously thinking—this is because our bodies react to emotions before our conscious mind becomes aware of them. We are also generally much better at reading the body language of someone we know well because the familiarity allows us to build a better understanding of the subtle emotional cues that could be missed with people we don't know.

I know there is a lot to take in, but please don't over think it. We all have mirror neurons, a type of brain cell that responds equally whether we perform an action or we witness someone else perform the same action. Thanks to these mirror neurons, when you watch someone smile, the same neurons that would fire in your brain if you were smiling also activate. We're naturally equipped to read others' emotional states and intentions, so pay attention and be willing to trust your unconscious mind and your gut. If you can tune into your natural instincts, you're likely to be just as, if not more, effective than if you consciously analyse body language.

Shift your focus

Ultimately, when it comes to effective negotiation, we want to understand what's going on in the other person's head. It's a crucial skill to be able to influence effectively—we need to grasp what motivates the person across the table.

Often in negotiations, we get caught up in our own thoughts. We're wrapped up in our motivations, the pressures we're under, our concerns about how we're perceived and the fear of devaluing ourselves through our words and actions. We're preoccupied with what we stand to gain or lose, governed by our own deadlines and measures of success.

And guess what? The person we're negotiating with has a similar narrative playing in their head. Their concerns, pressures, motivations and goals might mirror ours more closely than we realise. Each of us, whether in a negotiation or in life, is trying to answer the same question: 'Am I valued?'

Over the years, I've learned the fastest route to manage your own discomfort is by focusing on the other party. If we're approaching conversations with the objective of creating value, then the reality is it's not about us. It wasn't until I left my corporate life and started my own business that I really learned about negotiating to create value.

For a lot of corporate businesses, negotiating price can be quite transactional. I spent seventeen years in finance, and despite believing I was highly relational in my corporate life, my true focus was on maximising the profitability of the businesses I worked for. I thought I was creating value in negotiations, but I was far more competitive than I wanted to acknowledge. I was extremely loyal to the businesses I worked for and, on reflection, I wasn't truly thinking holistically or considering the other party's needs, even if I thought I was.

Since embarking on my entrepreneurial journey, I've had to embrace being uncomfortable in ways I had never experienced in my corporate career. I walked away from a secure role with a highly lucrative salary and healthy bonus because, following a significant life event, I learned that I valued something greater. The most uncomfortable journey I've had is transitioning from my executive role in finance, where my identity and sense of worth was attached to the huge global brand names I worked for, to standing for my own value without having a globally recognised brand behind me.

When prospecting new business, I knew I couldn't compete with what larger companies bought to the table in terms of resources. And yet, for much of my early journey in business, I was in my own head focused on how I compared. Until I realised it wasn't about me, it wasn't about me proving my intrinsic value, that wasn't, and shouldn't have been, on the table.

It was always, and has always been, about the other party, not because they are more superior, but because I realised my extrinsic value is only meaningful in the context of their needs and interests. Until I invested in understanding them, I was limiting my opportunity to establish the value that was needed to be brought to the table and exchanged.

When trying to get into the other person's head, think about what makes them feel valued. Is it easing their pressure points? Meeting their metrics? Gaining recognition? Understanding these aspects can give you a significant advantage in the negotiation.

To do this effectively, you need to be fully present. It's not just about staying out of your head; it's about tuning into theirs. Ask probing questions, then listen—really listen. People often reveal more than they intend through their words and actions. And sometimes, what they don't say is just as important as what they do.

In summary, you give life to what you give energy. By shifting your focus to the other party and understanding what they value, you can grow your extrinsic value, which is only valuable when it's considered in the context of others' needs.

Negotiation nuggets:
U — Embrace feeling uncomfortable

- *Growth through discomfort*: Realise that stepping out of your comfort zone is where you'll grow the most in your negotiation abilities. It's often those uneasy moments that teach us the most.

- *Down sides of comfort seeking*: Be aware that always seeking comfort can lead to missed opportunities. There's a lot to gain from taking risks and facing challenging situations head on.

- *Preparation and practise are key*: Underline the importance of being well-prepared and practising, especially the parts that make you squirm a bit. This builds confidence and skill.

- *Information gathering is crucial*: Don't shy away from asking those hard questions. Every piece of information you gather can give you an edge in negotiations.

- *Tough questions offer opportunities*: Change how you view difficult questions. Rather than dreading them, see them as chances to get a better deal.

- *Choose your words wisely*: Pay close attention to your language. The right words can strengthen your position, while the wrong ones can weaken it.

- *Silence is a strategy*: Learn to use silence effectively. It's not just a pause but a powerful tool that can help in gathering thoughts and insights.

- *Body language matters*: Be mindful of your non-verbal cues. They can convey a lot about your confidence and control in the negotiation.

- *Focus on the other party too*: Shift some focus to understanding the other side's needs. This can lead to solutions that benefit everyone.

- *Stay present and engaged*: Finally, always be fully there in your negotiations. Listen actively and watch for non-verbal cues, as they can provide valuable insights.

Focus five action list: Embrace feeling uncomfortable

Action	Activity	Done
Prepare tough questions	Before your next negotiation, write down a list of questions that make you feel uncomfortable. These are often the most critical and can produce the most valuable information.	
Practise discomfort	Engage in role-playing exercises with a friend or colleague, focusing on asking tough questions and navigating uncomfortable scenarios.	
Shift your language	Replace loose language with firm, assertive statements. Instead of saying, 'Ideally, I would like to…', say, 'My requirement is…'.	
Embrace silence	After presenting your proposal, resist the urge to fill the silence. Allow a pause and observe the other person's reactions.	
Observe body language	Pay attention to your own and the other party's body language. Look for self-soothing gestures, mismatches between words and gestures, and other non-verbal cues.	

Chapter 11

E — Execute the plan

The fifth and final key to becoming an effective negotiator is to execute the plan. A plan without execution is like having a battery without a device, it's packed with energy, but nothing gets powered! This chapter is your call to action to move forward and put into practise everything you've learned thus far.

Adaptability will be key, because even with a clear plan it's highly likely that something you haven't anticipated will come up. At this point you may be wondering what the point of a plan is if you're likely to be surprised with something new? And you wouldn't be the only one thinking that, or going into a negotiation choosing to wing it and see what happens.

I hope through what I've shared so far that you'll be someone who chooses differently. I know it's easy to dismiss the value of a plan if the reality you experience is expected to be different. When I was working in finance, I had many people tell me they didn't see the point of the budget because 'we were never going to hit it'. But what most people don't understand about budgets is that it's never about the budget, it's about discovering what the business could become and achieve by going through the planning process and considering what's possible.

It's the same with your negotiation plan, it's not about the plan per se, but about you. It's about who you are going to become and what you are going to achieve by going through the process of planning and then executing it. In this chapter I'll take you through how to execute the plan so that you have clarity on what you need to consider before, during and after the negotiation.

The power of intention

For many years, I didn't write down my goals. As time passed, I would reflect and make a cursory assessment of whether it had been a good year based on what I achieved, but I had no clear idea whether my achievements were bringing me closer to who I wanted to become because I wasn't being intentional. This lack of intention has cost me a lot over the years in terms of wasted time, energy and money.

Perhaps you see this lack of intention in your daily life too? Do you receive meeting invites without an agenda? Are the meetings you attend defined by clear objectives and success criteria? Do you find yourself losing time to competing priorities?

The knock-on effects of not being intentional are significant. On page 12, I shared that the core distinction between a regular conversation to reach an agreement and a negotiation is intention.

Most people won't be intentional with their planning or their execution, and what you choose to do next is entirely up to you.

One thing I've learned, both in business and in life, is that if you want access to the results that most people don't have, you have to do the things that most people won't do.

The path to our success first begins with our intention.

Pre-negotiation

When it comes to executing your plan, the key priority prior to the negotiation is to intentionally set the scene so that when you're at the table things go as smoothly as possible.

Setting up the negotiation involves appropriately priming the other party and positioning your value in advance.

Priming is a psychological concept that subtly shapes perceptions, attitudes and behaviours. For example, if one of your colleagues shares a negative experience about working with a retail buyer who is now responsible for purchasing the products you sell, you'll have subtly been primed to be cautious and possibly expect a challenging first meeting. If your colleague's view is accurate, then this may be helpful; however, if it's not, you could inadvertently find yourself communicating based on the priming you had.

It's important to think about how you want to prime the other party so that their perception is conducive to helping you gain the agreement you seek. There are many ways you could do this including:

- *Setting up a pre-meeting:* Arranging a call or a meeting to build rapport in advance of the negotiation can be an effective method to help you learn more about each other and appropriately prime the other party on what they can expect. You can carefully position your priorities without getting into the negotiation itself, setting a positive tone and easing any initial tensions.

- *Provide pre-negotiation materials:* Sending through pre-reading materials could include research, social proof of your company's existing track record through testimonials and case studies, or demonstrating your credibility or authority through whitepapers.

- *Choosing the environment:* We've already discussed on page 112 how the choice of environment can influence the tone of the negotiation and it's important to give this consideration.

- *Setting an agenda:* This will help you to structure the meeting and prime expectations.

Other ways to prime include leveraging people and published data sources (see page 162) that align with your positioning. In high stake negotiations, it is expected that stakeholders who are influential in the negotiation will be primed and aligned in advance to ensure the opportunity to secure agreement is maximised.

By thoughtfully priming the other party and positioning your value beforehand, you create a favourable atmosphere that can lead to more productive and positive negotiations.

During the negotiation

We usually have impressions in our minds of what negotiations look like based on television shows and movies. We hear stories of unique negotiation situations that are not everyday negotiations (unless you are in the police force), like kidnappings and hostage situations, and they sound dramatic and intense. The reality for most business and personal negotiations is not that dramatic.

What happens in the negotiation itself comes down to three critical activities: making proposals, countering proposals and then agreeing. I appreciate I've made this sound rather simple and yet it is the crux of what needs to happen when we're at the negotiating table.

Negotiations often become long and protracted because parties become entrenched in their positions or trying to prove how 'right' their position is. We've all had conversations trying to reach an agreement where our assessment of the data and situation has differed from the other party's. If we let our Joker out to play, it's likely that it'll seek to try and convince the other party that our assessment of the situation is more accurate than theirs.

The fastest way to get someone entrenched in their position is to tell them they are wrong. As we learned from the consistency principle, people seek to stay consistent with what they've previously said or done, so to try and get them to move from their position by forcing your opinions on them isn't the answer. Two Jokers at the table aren't going to maximise the value available in a deal.

Don't get drawn into debates or trying to 'sell' your position, by doing so you weaken your effectiveness in securing a more valuable agreement. Debates are essentially forms of arguments and we know they aren't effective because we see politicians spend more of their time postering in debates than we see them effectively create value for all their constituents.

When it comes to making an agreement, before you say 'yes', assess if your decision is driven by a desire for relief from discomfort or because the offer is genuinely within an acceptable range. It's easy to accept deals that haven't been fully explored and, therefore, haven't maximised the available value because we often choose comfort over discomfort. If you agree too quickly, you might later realise that you succumbed to your comfort zone and settled for less than what might have been available. Always strive to ensure that your acceptance is based on the true potential of the deal, not just a rush to alleviate unease.

How you make and receive proposals

I often get asked who should make the first proposal and my answer is that it depends, and there is no one strategy that fits every scenario. Typically, in a business context, where you already have knowledge of the market and can make a robust assessment of value based on the data you've gathered, I would encourage you to make the first proposal.

The psychological effect of anchoring is incredibly strong, which means that, subconsciously, the first offer on the table often becomes a reference point for the rest of the negotiation. It's like when an anchor is dropped from a boat; the distance the boat moves is relative to where the anchor was dropped. While most people think they are immune to the effects of anchoring because they are aware of the concept, the likelihood is that you won't be and there will be a subconscious anchor to the proposal that was first presented.

If the other party puts forward their proposal first, and it's a low offer, it's hard not to feel that you need to focus on pulling them up from their position. We end up having their number in mind and then our strategy becomes focused on trying to move them from their anchor position rather than focusing on presenting our own position. If the other party presents their proposal first, you may need to consciously flip your reference point for the negotiation to be your proposal not theirs. For example, you're seeking sponsorship for an event and you're in negotiation with a potential sponsor who says they only have $5000 (their anchor) to spend, but your packages start from $20 000. It's easy to feel that you need to convince them to come up because they mentioned their number (dropped their anchor) first. If you flip your reference point and keep focused on the fact that your packages start at $20 000 whenever you present options, it's with this reference point in mind, because you move from your starting point not theirs. Be mindful that your actions can also reinforce the anchoring effect—just the act of repeating their proposals back to them, even if it is to clarify that you've heard it correctly, can have an adverse effect of anchoring the other party's proposal in your mind.

Whenever you're making counter proposals, it's important to acknowledge for yourself that you are always moving from *your* last proposal not *their* last proposal. This approach ensures that you maintain focus on your objectives rather than being swayed by the other party's anchor point. For instance, if you initially offer a product for $10 000 and the buyer counters with $6000, instead of being pulled towards their low offer, you should consider your next move based on your original position. You might counter with $9000, showing that while you're open to negotiating, you're not anchored to their $6000 offer. They might come back with $7000, but that doesn't mean your next move needs to be $8000 because of this new anchor. You might choose to make a move to $8500.

By planning your moves and consistently countering from your last proposal, you can make strategic concession that align with your goals and avoid unnecessary concessions. Often the proposals the other party makes are not exactly the proposals that we expect. It's important to be mindful that, regardless of their proposals, unless it's a better proposal, you can continue to stick to your plan and counter with your planned next proposal.

Until we've got an acceptable deal, we want to keep the conversation going, and often it's easy to fall into rejecting a proposal because it's not what we want. It's important to avoid triggering the other party into wanting to retaliate because we've made a direct rejection of their proposal. Remember, we all want to know we are being valued, which is why rejection hurts. Instead of challenging or rejecting their proposal, thank them for their proposal and, instead of saying what you can't agree on, tell them what you can agree to by offering a counter proposal of your own.

Etiquette when receiving proposals is to never interrupt the other party when they are making a proposal. If you interrupt them, you fail to see what they would have given you, and by interrupting you're also missing the opportunity to strengthen relationships. No-one likes being interrupted when they are speaking and it can do more harm than good.

Please also don't ask someone for their best offer. Negotiation is a ritual—each party has moves they are going to make. If you ask them to show you their best move right up front, you leave them nowhere to go in the process and it's highly unlikely they are going to give you the very best offer they can give right from the beginning. Don't kill the deal before you've honoured the ritual of exchanging value.

Be persuadable

To effectively persuade others, you must first be open to persuasion yourself. Negotiations, whether personal or professional, tend to stall when you expect the other party to do something that you are not demonstrating yourself. If you want someone to move from their position towards yours, show that you're willing to do the same; for example, if you're negotiating a business contract and want the other party to consider a more flexible timeline, start by showing your willingness to adjust other terms of the contract that matter to them.

Use the reciprocity principle of influence we spoke about on page 208. When you give something, the other party is likely to want to give something in return—it's a universal norm. Under pressure, we might find ourselves focusing on our own perspectives and not enough on understanding others'. To begin to influence others effectively, pay attention to their needs and interests, not just your own.

How to exchange value

When it comes to creating value, focus on the low cost, high perceived value exchange approach. This involves offering something that costs you little but is perceived as highly valuable by the other party. For example, in a partnership deal, you may offer to share your extensive network of industry contacts. This costs you little in terms of effort, but could be highly valuable to the other party. In return, you receive something that holds high value for you but is low cost for them to give. Remember, *cost* doesn't always refer to money; it can also mean time, energy or other resources. This approach requires making offers that are conditional, expecting a reciprocal exchange.

By being conditional in our offers, we encourage a balanced give and take, honouring the value both parties bring to the table. It's important to recognise that people often do not appreciate what they receive for free, which can lead to feelings of greed or entitlement. By focusing on a value exchange and avoiding giving anything away for free, you teach the other party to value your contributions. We tend to value things we've worked hard to obtain more than those that come easily. Therefore, let the other party work for a good deal, enhancing their appreciation of the value once it's agreed upon. If you want to give something away for free, then make sure you treat it as a genuine gift. Label it as such and don't expect anything in return.

When we haven't appropriately exchanged value, it's easy to fall into the trap of blaming the other party. I've heard many people try to convince the other party how much they've already moved and highlight how much less the other party has moved, often to encourage them to move and give up something. Negotiating isn't about splitting the difference, reaching a mid-point or being fair. If you've moved more than you were comfortable moving, then you either didn't make the proposal conditional and didn't link it to an exchange of value, or you are caught in the fallacy of fairness. Either way, that's not the other party's responsibility, it's yours.

If you make your exchanges conditional, then it becomes easier for both parties to keep repackaging the overall deal until you find a solution that's acceptable to both.

Taking notes in a negotiation

If you took notes during your negotiation conversation, what would they tell me? We know analysing the data is a significant key to unlocking value and yet we leave so much data that's available uncaptured. While it would be expected in a business negotiation to note down the proposals that have been made by the other party, most people don't take a moment to note down how they were made and when they were made.

The more effective our notes are, the more data we have to be able to understand the other party and influence them towards a more valuable agreement. As I mentioned in Chapter 8, people are a significant source of data. What words did the other party use when delivering their proposal or responding to you? Was their language loose or tight? Did their body language consistently match their words or were there inconsistencies? Did their tone change when delivering their proposals versus the moments prior? Did they look comfortable, or did you notice anything that indicated they were uncomfortable?

Did they mention any data sources—people or published data that would be useful for you to remember? Did they give you information that would help you build greater depth in your connection, such as their partner or children's names, the way they take their coffee? It can seem overwhelming at first to capture notes that are effective, but over time it can become an incredibly valuable source of insight that helps strengthen relationships and create mutual value.

To give some structure on how you could organise your notes table 11.1 shows a suggestion.

Table 11.1   how to take notes in a negotiation

Discussion points and agreements	Interests and objectives
<ul><li>agenda items</li><li>offers and counter offers</li><li>agreed points and action items</li><li>follow-up items</li><li>next steps and deadlines</li></ul>	<ul><li>key concerns and interests</li><li>potential obstacles and solutions</li><li>values and priorities</li></ul>
Rapport and relationships	**Observational insights**
<ul><li>common ground and interests</li><li>personal details</li><li>communication and feedback</li></ul>	<ul><li>non-verbal cues and emotional responses</li><li>cultural or organisational insights</li><li>emotional and behavioural insights</li></ul>
Reflection and strategy	
<ul><li>questions and clarifications</li><li>personal reflections and insights</li><li>feedback and compliments</li></ul>	

How to avoid conversations stalling or people being entrenched in their positions

While we will have already considered who's at the table and have prepared as best we can for the potential uninvited guests that may turn up when stress levels increase and buttons are pressed, it's important we manage the climate so that we prevent, as best we can, the discussions getting heated. Managing the climate of the conversation keeps it conducive to getting the outcome we seek. This means we must consciously ensure our behaviour is appropriate to the circumstances, that our tone is monitored and that the words we use are positive and focused towards reaching a mutually beneficial outcome. Don't destroy the trust in a relationship by using negative, abrasive or oppositional language. Nobody wants to work with a jerk. Our memories are long, and the world is too small and, frankly, karma's not an opponent you want to challenge.

Ultimately, each party must walk away feeling satisfied at end of the deal because, unless they do, there is a risk that the deal just agreed on could be renegaded on. When it comes to negotiating, we're having conversations to reach an agreement; it's not about winning a competition.

Time out

As I mentioned on page 178, it's more than likely that you'll receive information during a negotiation that you may not be expecting. When this happens, it's okay to take a time out, if needed, to gather your thoughts. The worst thing you can do is continue with the conversation and try to think and talk at the same time. This only leads to loose language leaking value (see page 216 for a refresher), so it's important to get clear on how you need to move forward before you continue negotiating.

Asking for time out can feel uncomfortable, but it's important to remember that you want to always be in your power and never feel powerless. Remember your ACE and allow yourself the opportunity to be the best you can be—when you feel doubt, take a time out.

If it's not possible to leave the room for whatever reason, you can take a time out with a pause and the use of silence. Signal that you're taking a moment and let the other party wait while you regroup. The use of pausing and silence is appropriate to keep the conversation productive and your Joker out of the dialogue.

Summarise often

During the negotiation, keeping everyone clear on how the conversation is progressing and in what areas each party are aligned on is critical, and so frequent pauses to summarise is necessary and recommended. Especially if the negotiation is lengthy and conducted over multiple interactions, it's important to summarise often so that there is no misalignment. I use the word *alignment* deliberately, rather than agreement, because in negotiations involving multiple variables, it's necessary to keep everything in play until you have alignment on a total package you can say 'yes' to. It's only once you're aligned across all variables that you can say: 'Yes, we have reached an agreement.'

After the negotiation

As I've mentioned previously, the negotiation doesn't end when you walk out of the room. There are a number of steps you need to take to ensure you not only achieved the outcome you were after, but that you also record the necessary information for future interactions.

Review and implementation

Unless you look back, it's hard to know how far you've come. Ultimately, if we value growth, then taking time to reflect and review how things went is important. It's easy to miss this step, after all the agreement has been made, that's success, right? Perhaps, but I'd like to know if I could replicate that success and whether I could create even more value next time.

As with everything, it depends on what you value. Do you value long-term growth or the transaction? Do you value continuous improvement or comfort? When reviewing the negotiation, understand what went well and what didn't go well. Consider what changes you would need to make and what you would do differently next time.

Don't forget what happens next

Usually, agreement is the first step and there are follow-up actions required—what did you note down regarding implementation? What needs to happen next?

In business deals, we must ensure what was agreed on is followed through, that the value we expected is realised. This may involve measuring the key performance indicators of the deal, it could include quarterly check-ins to ensure the terms of the agreement are being complied with, it could include understanding what events would trigger a renegotiation. Do you know who's responsible for managing the performance of the agreement and what the escalation points are?

Celebrate

Finally, we celebrate! Celebration is not just due to the tangible successes or the outcomes you achieved, nor just for the value created through the relationships you've developed, but most importantly, for who you became through this journey.

Negotiating isn't easy—it challenges you to step out of your comfort zone, embrace discomfort and lean in when it is hardest. In doing so, you access the part of yourself that you can trust, the part of you that has your back, whatever the situation.

When you recognise that the true value you create is more than just reaching an agreement—it's about the legacy you leave by building value, not destroying it—you see that value negotiation isn't just something that you do, it's who you become through the process.

Negotiation nuggets:
E — Execute the plan

Phase 1: Pre-negotiation

- *Strategic preparation*: Start by diving deep into the 6 W's (Why, Who, What, When, Where, Which) to fully grasp the context of your negotiation. This groundwork helps you strategise effectively and set a solid foundation.

- *Value identification and data analysis*: Focus on uncovering what each party values. Analyse the data thoroughly to prepare for making strong, informed proposals that resonate with all sides.

- *Leverage and power*: Understand your leverage — both real and perceived. Use this insight to guide the negotiation thoughtfully and ethically, maximising outcomes while maintaining integrity.

Phase 2: During the negotiation

- *Execute with adaptability*: Implement your plan flexibly, adjusting your strategies as needed based on how the negotiation evolves. Make proposals thoughtfully and handle counterproposals with care.

- *Communicate effectively*: Use clear and persuasive communication. Show openness to adapting your stance, encouraging the other party to do the same, which helps build trust and cooperation.

- *Manage proposals*: Approach proposal dynamics cautiously. Set a strong starting point with your initial proposal to anchor the discussion effectively and be conscious of how anchoring biases might influence responses.

Phase 3: After the negotiation

- *Document and manage data*: Carefully document the outcomes and manage your data meticulously to keep valuable insights accessible for ongoing use and analysis.

- *Review and adjust*: Regularly review the agreement and its real-world application to ensure it continues to meet the business needs effectively. Adjust as necessary to align with ongoing goals and conditions.

- *Reflect for growth*: Take time to reflect on the negotiation process. Identify what went well and what could be improved. Use these insights to refine your approach for even better results in future negotiations.

Focus five action list: Execute the plan

Action	Activity	Done
Set clear intentions	Write down your goals and the desired outcomes for your negotiation before starting. Be specific about what you want to achieve and who you want to become through the process.	
Prime the other party	Use pre-meeting calls, pre-negotiation materials and setting a structured agenda to prepare the other party and position your value in advance.	
Anchor your proposals	Make the first proposal, where appropriate, to leverage the psychological effect of anchoring. If the other party makes the first proposal, consciously flip your reference point to your own position.	
Use conditional offers	Make offers that are conditional on receiving something of value in return. Avoid giving away anything for free and, instead, structure exchanges to emphasise the value you bring.	
Review and reflect	After each negotiation, take time to review what went well and what didn't. Consider what changes you would make and how you can create more value next time.	

Chapter 12

Values for successful negotiation

In laying the foundations for value-driven negotiations and applying the Value Method, you've significantly advanced your negotiation intelligence. However, as I've often emphasised, negotiation isn't just about the skills you develop—it's about who you become through the process. Those who are successful in negotiations set themselves apart by embodying essential values—values that enhance their emotional intelligence and define their character as a Value Negotiator.

The person we negotiate with most is ourselves. Our values act as shortcuts to remember who we aspire to be in our negotiations, guiding our behaviour and reminding us of the impact we can choose to have on the world through the way we act. Observing these values helps us to navigate the fine line between assertiveness and aggression, leading to outcomes that are both positive and sustainable.

They ensure we remain on the right side of power versus force and build relationships that endure beyond the negotiating table.

If you've ever experienced a deadlock or stalemate, you'll know how frustrating it is to feel stuck when you're at an impasse. Whether in our professional or personal lives, reaching this point can seem like a dead end, making it difficult to see a path forward.

The value of creativity isn't just about getting unstuck in negotiations; it's about unlocking potential and accessing value that might otherwise remain out of reach. In negotiations, creativity isn't optional; it's critical. As Einstein famously remarked, 'The definition of insanity is doing the same thing over and over again, but expecting different results'.

We're going to look at six values: creativity, connection, curiosity, compassion, care and contribution. These values will equip you to thrive in any negotiation scenario and 'C's' opportunities with integrity.

Each value has a distinct objective:

- *Creativity:* transform challenges into shared rewards

- *Connection:* value relationships over transactions

- *Curiosity:* explore deeper to solve smarter

- *Compassion:* drive every deal with understanding

- *Care:* ensure that both relationships and results matter

- *Contribution:* make a meaningful impact, not just participation.

By the end of this chapter, I hope you'll recognise that by honing and applying these values, you not only boost your confidence in any negotiation scenario, but also significantly elevate the quality of your outcomes. This enhancement comes through developing your emotional intelligence and establishing your identity as a Value Negotiator.

How much is enough?

As we reflect on these six values, another critical question arises: 'How much is enough?' In a world that constantly pushes us for more, this question becomes increasingly relevant and complex.

I watched a reality TV show that perfectly captured this dilemma. In the show, $250 000 was divided equally among eleven contestants who were living together in a luxurious house. The rules were simple: no-one had to be voted out. If everyone remained unanimous, they would all leave with an equal share of the prize.

In the first public voting ceremony, unsurprisingly, the contestants unanimously chose not to vote anyone out, a decision that was met with their collective celebration. But as we know, reality TV thrives on drama, and the voting rules changed. Subsequent votes were cast in private, one by one, unravelling the dynamics within the group. Alliances formed and judgements about each contestant's deservingness came into play. One contestant was voted out simply because he revealed that he was already a millionaire, and others felt he didn't need the money.

The game introduced various temptations, allowing contestants to secretly take money from the communal pot, which reduced what was available to others. Strategies varied widely: some contestants acted with integrity, while others, driven by their personal and family needs, resorted to manipulation to get as much money as they could. The relationships and collective wellbeing in the house became secondary to individual gains. By the time the final episode rolled around, only five contestants were left, each with a different portion of the money determined by their actions and choices throughout the game.

Watching this, I was fascinated by how negotiations are deeply influenced by our individual values, morals and ethics. Greed and trust play significant roles, with some individuals focused entirely on personal gain, while others considered the collective benefit, aiming for a deal that worked well for everyone.

As you navigate your own negotiations, how you choose to carry yourself is crucial. Through understanding and applying the six values, my hope is that you'll consciously choose how to show up and engage in situations designed to test you under pressure. This understanding not only helps answer 'How much is enough?' but also shapes the way we approach both life's opportunities and its challenges.

The value of creativity

Post-university, I began my professional career as a chartered management accountant. I had the privilege of working for large global corporations and, over the years, I collaborated with many different people across various functions, countries and backgrounds. Aside from the usual jokes most finance folks hear about being 'creative' with numbers, it wasn't common, in my experience, to hear the finance function described as a bunch of creative people.

Creativity is the key that opens doors we didn't even know existed.

Often our perspectives of what it means to be creative are distorted by our environment and associated biases, which is why I want to address three common misconceptions.

Misconception 1: Creativity is only for 'creative types'

It's a myth that creativity is reserved for certain personalities. This was certainly a belief I once held, but creativity is a skill that anyone can develop. It arises from the willingness to view problems from multiple angles and to consider a range of solutions. Regardless of your role at work or home, creativity is an essential value for solving problems and identifying solutions.

Misconception 2: Creativity complicates things

Many people assume that creativity introduces complexity due to its unstructured nature. Yet, in my experience, creativity often streamlines problem-solving. It reveals simpler and more effective solutions, especially in negotiations, where it can turn a deadlock into a pathway for consensus.

Take, for example, a tenant and landlord negotiating a lease renewal. To address the tenant's concern about rising costs and the landlord's worry about vacancy, the tenant proposes prepaying six months of rent for a reduced monthly rate. This solution provides immediate cash flow to the landlord and lowers the tenant's expenses, resolving the deadlock and benefiting both parties.

Misconception 3: Creativity is inappropriate in serious situations

Our biases about creativity often lead us to believe it has no place in serious contexts, causing us hesitation in sharing creative ideas in high-stakes meetings. Yet, creativity is crucial in these scenarios, particularly when conventional approaches fall short. It facilitates the discovery of innovative solutions that effectively address critical needs and solve complex problems.

In negotiations, effectively maximising value is impossible without creativity. Although we are encouraged to think outside the box, our work environment, risk appetite and often narrow perspectives limit our ability to discover new possibilities. Additionally, as adults, our reduced engagement in play and imagination means our creativity muscle isn't always as strong as it could be, further constraining our innovative potential.

How to leverage creativity in negotiations

Leveraging creativity becomes effortless when we intentionally create the space for others to share their perspectives and allow for unconventional thinking and activities to inspire ideas.

Encourage diverse perspectives

Involve multiple stakeholders, such as impact bearers, internal and external stakeholders and decisions-makers—or a combination of these functions—in your negotiation process. Different viewpoints can inspire unique solutions that you might not consider on your own. This diversity enriches the pool of ideas and fosters innovation.

Use brainstorming techniques

Implement structured brainstorming sessions during your negotiations. Encourage all participants to freely share ideas without immediate critique, creating an environment where innovative and unconventional ideas can flourish.

Incorporate elements of play

Introduce playful activities or exercises as part of your negotiation planning process. These can help break down barriers and stimulate creative thinking in a relaxed atmosphere. Techniques such as role-playing scenarios or creative problem-solving games can stimulate discussions and lead to unexpected insights.

Be flexible with proposals

Maintain flexibility in adjusting your proposals as negotiations evolve. This adaptability allows for creative compromises that meet the needs of and satisfy all parties involved.

The value in creativity is limitless. The challenge we have is in recognising our own capability when it comes to being creative, and developing our capacity in the way in which we are leveraging creativity to create mutually beneficial outcomes.

The value of connection

Have you ever been ghosted? Originally a term from the dating world, 'ghosting' (suddenly cutting off all communication without explanation) has become prevalent in various types of relationships, including professional ones. Have you communicated with a potential prospect, held discovery meetings and sent proposals, only to have them disappear when decisions need to be made?

What most people fail to realise is that ghosting is a symptom of a major pandemic the world is facing—a communication pandemic. The inability to acknowledge someone's messages goes beyond just avoidance, being too busy or being distracted; it's a symptom of our discomfort with communicating our needs and boundaries. It represents a disconnection from ourselves as much as from others.

This disconnection has a knock-on effect on our ability to negotiate. You can't negotiate effectively if you can't, or won't, connect with yourself and others.

The value of connection goes beyond just building rapport; it involves recognising our shared humanity and understanding how small acts of disconnection, like failing to communicate properly, can lead to dehumanising behaviour. When we neglect the value of connection, we risk damaging relationships, tarnishing our reputation and compromising our integrity.

Valuing connection means treating others as we would like to be treated. It doesn't require responding to every unsolicited email, but it does mean engaging respectfully and closing loops with those we interact with. The more we do this, the more we strengthen our connection with ourselves, our leadership and elevate the standards of communication we give and accept from others.

How to build connection

Building connection is at the heart of effective negotiation where self-awareness, prioritising people, authenticity and consistent communication lay the foundations for strong relationships.

Cultivate self-awareness

Develop your emotional intelligence by engaging in self-reflection. Ask yourself questions, such as:

- What am I feeling and why?

- What am I avoiding and why?

- What are my underlying motivations in this negotiation?

This will help you understand your own emotions, motivations and values. This self-awareness enriches your interactions in negotiations and allows for more intentional rather than unconscious responses.

Prioritise people

Acknowledge the human element in every negotiation. You are dealing with individuals who have emotions, aspirations and concerns.

Recognising this is the first step towards building a genuine connection.

Build trust through authenticity

Engage authentically with everyone you meet. Trust is the cornerstone of any meaningful relationship and cannot be built on insincerity. Being genuine in your interactions fosters trust and opens communication channels.

Maintain consistent communication

Ensure that the channels of communication remain open before, during and after negotiations. Consistency in communication not only shows commitment, but also strengthens relationships and builds a foundation for future interactions.

◆ ◆ ◆

These principles aren't easy to embrace in a world that accepts standards that are much lower. However, the values we embrace are there to remind us of the person we aspire to be and the minimum standard we want to set for ourselves. How will you leverage connection to improve both your personal and professional interactions?

The value of curiosity

Curiosity is an inherent part of our nature, which was vibrant and evident in our early years as we incessantly questioned our parents and tried to make sense of the world around us. However, as we grow older, our innate curiosity often diminishes. It might be quenched by the constant flow of information, or perhaps we learn to suppress it after being told it's inappropriate to probe too deeply. Sometimes, curiosity might even lead us into trouble or, worse still, the belief that curiosity killed the cat, as the old saying goes, pairing fear with our desire to know more, causing us to hold back.

There are numerous reasons why our curiosity fades: we're exhausted, overwhelmed, trying to keep pace in a fast-moving world or bombarded by so much information that we can't possibly absorb any more. I often ponder whether the world is facing a curiosity crisis. Algorithms shape our digital landscapes, ensuring we only encounter information that aligns with our existing interests, turning our social feeds into echo chambers filled with the familiar. This curated exposure compromises our ability to explore deeply and solve problems more effectively—we simply don't realise what we're missing.

True wisdom lies in seeking, not just in knowing.

In my training sessions, I see that many people believe that they need to be a subject matter expert before they can ask 'intelligent' questions. This belief is flawed as is trying to boost confidence through knowledge alone, being afraid of appearing uninformed or making mistakes. This fear of devaluing oneself leads people to play it safe, holding back and limiting their own growth. A better approach is reconnecting with your curiosity. Being curious provides leverage—not knowing all the answers is fine as long as you ask the right questions.

In leadership, the most effective CEOs I've worked with excel in asking pertinent questions that help in gathering information and making decisions. This is equally vital in negotiation. When you have a high self-regard and emotional intelligence, you stop worrying about others' perceptions and focus on asking questions that reveal underlying problems and facilitate the discovery of optimal solutions.

My ability to work effectively with clients across various industries and serve as a non-executive board director of a non-profit is not due to my having expertise in every field. It's because I've nurtured my curiosity about people, analysed published data and spent time honing my questioning and listening skills. This has enhanced my problem-solving capabilities and my ability to identify effective solutions.

Curiosity doesn't just help with problem-solving; it also helps you to suspend judgement of people and their actions, and prevents you from jumping to conclusions based on false assumptions. If someone does something you don't understand, choose curiosity over judgement. This approach is especially beneficial in conflict situations, where keeping an open mind promotes understanding rather than quick judgements.

By cultivating your curiosity, you will deepen your connections, build trust and enhance your creativity, allowing you to connect dots that others might miss.

How to develop your curiosity

Developing curiosity in negotiations not only enriches your understanding, but also creates a more dynamic and innovative approach to identifying solutions.

Ask open-ended questions

Cultivate an environment where your open-ended questions, such as, 'What are your primary concerns about this proposal?' or 'How do you see the solution working?' Encourage a comprehensive exchange of ideas instead of using closed questions; for example, 'Do you agree with this proposal?' This approach not only gathers more information, but also signals your genuine interest in understanding others' perspectives.

Embrace active listening

Practise active listening, which goes hand-in-hand with curiosity. Listen not just to respond, but to truly understand, which can often lead to breakthroughs in deadlocked situations, especially because in these situations most people are more concerned with getting their point across. You no longer need to think of questions, the questions will naturally arise from your presence and curiosity.

Challenge the status quo

Use your curiosity to challenge the usual ways of doing things. Enquire why certain procedures are followed and whether alternative methods might yield better results.

In negotiations, the more you say, the more you give away and the less you learn. Instead, use your curiosity with questions like, 'Can you tell me more about....?' to understand the people and the situation more deeply than anyone else, allowing you to navigate the negotiation with insight and clarity.

The value of compassion

Are you a compassionate person? In negotiation, compassion is often misunderstood. While empathy is widely recognised as essential for understanding the needs and interests of others, compassion can sometimes be seen as a vulnerability, especially in competitive or adversarial environments. Yet, integrating compassion enhances your emotional intelligence, bringing a critical dimension to negotiations.

Compassion in negotiation is about more than understanding — it's about actionable empathy.

Figure 12.1 explores the distinctions between sympathy, empathy and compassion.

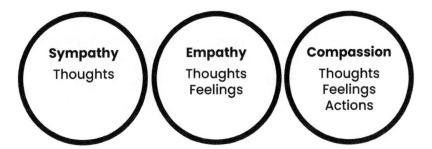

Figure 12.1 the distinctions between sympathy, empathy and compassion

- *Sympathy* involves acknowledging another's difficulties from a distance, offering condolences or polite concern without truly feeling what they feel: 'I'm sorry you're having a difficult time. I'm thinking of you.'

- *Empathy* is a core component of emotional intelligence that deepens your connection, allowing you to genuinely feel and understand what another person is experiencing. This understanding is then reflected in your negotiation approach: 'I understand what you must be feeling and I can empathise.' One of the best exercises I completed in developing deep empathy was seeking to understand why someone would do something I would never do. I chose to practise having empathy for a smoker. As someone who has never once tried smoking, I couldn't understand why anyone would, until I put myself in the shoes of a smoker and imagined the thoughts they might think and the feelings they might feel. That one exercise deepened my ability to connect without judgement.

- *Compassion* takes empathy further by actively seeking to alleviate others' difficulties. It means you not only understand their situation, but are also compelled to help improve it. Integrating compassion into negotiation doesn't mean compromising your goals or forsaking professional boundaries; it means using wisdom and good judgement to discover solutions that benefit all parties involved: 'I understand what you must be experiencing; how can I best help?'

Being compassionate elevates our humanity. In a world rife with competitiveness and transactional interactions, empathy provides understanding, but it doesn't always lead to action. Compassion, however, transforms empathy into practical steps that enhance outcomes for both ourselves and others.

In the high-pressure context of negotiation, the fear of devaluing oneself might drive us to prioritise our own outcomes over others'. This focus can make it challenging to embrace compassion. This is why being a compassionate negotiator is crucial, not only in negotiation, but in broader leadership situations. Compassionate leadership means anticipating concerns, recognising fears and addressing them constructively. It demonstrates that understanding and consideration can coexist with achieving ambitious goals. In high-stakes environments, showing compassion ensures that the people you work with are supported to thrive, not just to survive under pressure.

How to use compassion in negotiations

Integrating compassion into your negotiations strategies creates a more collaborative and non-judgemental environment, where empathy, acknowledgement of perspectives and equitable solutions are front of mind.

Lead with empathy

Start every negotiation by thoroughly understanding the other side's perspective. Ask open-ended questions that prompt comprehensive responses, such as, 'Can you share more about your priorities in this situation?' or 'What challenges are you currently facing?' and listen actively without judgement. This approach not only deepens your insight into their needs and concerns, but also sets a collaborative tone for the discussion.

Validate emotions and perspectives

Make it a point to acknowledge and validate the emotions and viewpoints of others. Doing so builds trust and opens lines of communication, which are crucial for navigating complex negotiations effectively. Use phrases like, 'It seems that you're feeling...,' 'It sounds like you're concerned about...,' or 'It looks like this issue is important to you...' to show that you recognise and respect their feelings and perspectives.

Advocate for equitable solutions

Once you have a clear understanding of the other side's needs, champion solutions that benefit all parties. Show that compassion in negotiations is about elevating everyone's interests, not just your own.

◆ ◆ ◆

Compassion may not be the most obvious value in negotiation, but it is a powerful one that can inspire positive actions. When you reflect on your past interactions, you will probably see that when you showed empathy and compassion you had more open and successful discussions. How will you bring compassion to enrich your negotiations or, if you are a manager, into your leadership approach?

The value of care

In my work life, I've often observed a strong commitment from myself and my colleagues to achieving optimal business outcomes. However, there are times when the focus on results overshadows the care needed for the people involved. Does this resonate with you? Have there been times when you've pushed for results over nurturing your relationship with friends, family or colleagues? In negotiations, genuinely caring means valuing both the results and the relationships you cultivate. This balanced approach is crucial because, while results are measurable, relationships are the foundation of long-term success. Achieving results in a way that respects and considers all parties involved is just as important as the outcomes themselves. In Chapter 2, we explored the different negotiator types—this is where The Diplomat archetype thrives, operating on the principle that care isn't about being soft, but about being respectful and considerate in the pursuit of outcomes.

Negotiation is the art of valuing results as much as relationships — both are non-negotiable.

In the commercial environments where many of us engage, care is often demonstrated in practical ways. For example, retailers frequently face demands for environmentally friendly products and increased consumer pressure to adopt more sustainable practices. These initiatives often involve costs related to upgrading machinery or changing materials, which can create points of contention. Although both parties typically agree on the goal of sustainable practices, the method of implementation requires thoughtful consideration. Demonstrations of care often include a phased implementation plan so suppliers aren't forced to write off old stock; incentives for early compliance to reward changes ahead of schedule; and extended contract terms to ensure business stability following significant capital investments by suppliers. This approach to care recognises that, although there are initial costs in the supply chain, creating sustainable practices should be managed thoughtfully and collaboratively, without undue pressure that disadvantages any party.

How to be caring in negotiations

Practising care in negotiations elevates our level of communication and fosters an environment where empathy, honesty and relationship building are prioritised.

Balance empathy with assertiveness

Practise empathy to fully understand the other party's needs while clearly communicating your own, ensuring solutions are respectful and mutually beneficial.

Foster long-term relationships

I've talked a lot about the value of relationships in negotiating terms that achieve a goal without breaking trust and relationships. It's important to negotiate with the future in mind, and to aim for outcomes that promote ongoing collaboration and trust.

Communicate openly and honestly

Be transparent about your objectives and constraints. Know the information you will openly give and what you will guard, saying, 'I'm sorry, I'm not able to share that specific information with you at this time, however, what I can share is...' will help, where appropriate, to protect your competitive advantage. This honesty fosters similar openness from others, leading to more authentic and effective negotiations.

◆ ◆ ◆

In negotiations, the focus on care is crucial to maximise outcomes while cultivating deeper and more meaningful relationships. Can you think about ways you might use care to create value in your negotiations? Obviously, it's easier to be caring in personal negotiations with family members and friends as it comes more naturally, however, we also need to bring care into the business environment with peers or counterparts—it simply requires us to be more creative!

The value of contribution

In Dr Martin Seligman's PERMA model, a framework for human flourishing within positive psychology, the 'M' represents *meaning*. It highlights our innate need for significance and purpose, which deeply influences our sense of self-worth and fulfilment. We often experience our greatest sense of value when we perceive our actions as contributing meaningfully to something greater than ourselves.

In successful negotiations, the same holds true. There's a significant difference between just showing up and making a real impact. Contribution is not just about what you bring to the discussion, but also about how you present yourself in those critical moments under pressure. By embodying the value of contribution, you aim to be impactful through your interactions, not just involved. This approach doesn't just change the outcomes of the negotiation—it transforms you, as a person, as well.

Real change is created by those who dare to contribute, not just participate.

Being a contributor means looking beyond your immediate desires and considering how you can help shape a better future for everyone. It's about creating a legacy of positive change where your actions speak volumes. Deep down, I believe we all recognise the value of making a difference, of contributing to something larger than ourselves. However, in negotiation this is more than altruism—making a contribution in the way you interact and give value to others is what creates more sustainable and profitable outcomes over the long term.

I often think about the future generations and how crucial negotiation skills will be in creating a world that builds value rather than diminishes it. With around one in three children and adolescents experiencing bullying in person and online and many women experiencing domestic violence, imagine the global impact if all children learned the skills of peaceful value negotiation at school. Enhancing communication capabilities and problem-solving skills, developing emotional intelligence (including greater self-awareness and improved emotional regulation) are just the start, and the long term, significant ripple effects on relationship skills, both at home and in the workplace, would be substantial.

Contribution as a value in negotiation prompts us to consider what can be collectively achieved when we share the goal of making a meaningful difference beyond individual gains. Imagine how a shared commitment to contribution could lead to monumental, global-scale outcomes.

In our daily personal and professional lives, the principle of contribution remains equally powerful. Choosing to be a contributor—whether by sharing your knowledge to enhance your friends' interactions or by engaging in sustainable practices with your customers and suppliers—elevates your role from a participant to a leader and changemaker. These actions not only influence immediate outcomes, but also contribute to a larger narrative of positive change, shaping your identity and legacy in significant ways.

How to make a contribution

In any negotiation, the essence of true contribution lies in the alignment of our actions with our values, leading by example and seeking to make a meaningful impact beyond the immediacy of the deal.

Align actions with values

Before entering any negotiation, take a moment to reflect on your core values and how you can align your contributions accordingly. This alignment with what you do and what you say is what defines your character and, ultimately, your legacy.

Lead by example

Demonstrate what it means to contribute positively by living the values you promote. This display of integrity and commitment serves as an inspiration, encouraging others to raise their standards. Remember, nothing changes if nothing changes.

Seek meaningful impact

Look beyond the surface of negotiations to understand how your contributions can create meaningful, lasting change. It's not just about the deal, it's about the difference the deal makes to everyone it touches.

◆ ◆ ◆

Embracing the value of contribution in negotiations challenges you to consider not only what you want, but also who you aspire to be. It urges you to be a leader of positive change, influencing not just the negotiation table, but extending far beyond it. What impact will you choose to make?

Negotiation nuggets:
Values for successful negotiation

- *Creativity*: Leverage creativity to turn negotiation challenges into opportunities for shared success. Push beyond the usual solutions to uncover innovative paths that benefit all parties.

- *Connection*: Prioritise deep, meaningful relationships over just transactional interactions. Strong connections are the foundation of trust and collaboration, essential for enduring success in negotiations.

- *Curiosity*: Actively seek deeper understanding and insights about others and circumstances. Use curiosity not just to gather information, but to challenge assumptions and drive negotiations smarter, more comprehensive solutions.

- *Compassion*: Employ compassion as a strategic tool in negotiations. By understanding and addressing the real needs of others, you create solutions that are not only effective, but also equitable and empathetic.

- *Care*: Balance achieving robust results with nurturing significant relationships. Show that true care in negotiations goes beyond niceties — it's about respect and integrity in every interaction.

- *Contribution*: Aim to be a catalyst for positive change. View each negotiation as an opportunity to contribute to something greater than the immediate deal, impacting the broader community and future generations.

Six core values to embody in value negotiation

Action	Activity	Done
Leverage creativity	Encourage diverse perspectives, use brainstorming techniques, incorporate elements of play and stay flexible with proposals.	
Build genuine connection	Cultivate self-awareness, prioritise people, build trust through authenticity and maintain consistent communication.	
Cultivate curiosity	Ask open-ended questions, embrace active listening, challenge the status quo and use curiosity to uncover deeper insights.	
Practise compassion	Lead with empathy, validate emotions and perspectives, and advocate for equitable solutions.	
Prioritise care	Balance empathy with assertiveness, foster long-term relationships and communicate openly and honestly.	
Make a meaningful contribution	Align actions with values, lead by example, and seek meaningful, lasting changes that benefit all parties involved.	

A final word

By choosing to develop your negotiation skills, you've not only enhanced your potential for better financial outcomes for yourself and your business, but also embarked on a journey to become a better leader and human being.

What I know for sure is that just reading this book won't be enough. Mastery in any field requires intentional practise. It's this intention that will shape the reality of your discipline, conscious choices and commitment to continual growth. I liken this to my daily practise of monitoring my thoughts to ensure they align with the future I want and the person I aspire to become.

Change stems from a deliberate choice about our identity. When you negotiate from this centred place, your decisions and actions will naturally align with your values, enhancing both the effectiveness and authenticity of your interactions.

It's vital to shift your mindset away from fears that stifle your creative potential. Being overly attached to a specific outcome can cloud your judgement and limit your ability to see alternative solutions. Practising detachment will help maintain flexibility and openness to new possibilities.

Remember, the person you negotiate with the most is yourself. If you can approach your inner dialogue with the same creativity, connection, curiosity, compassion, care and contribution that you bring to your external interactions, the value you cultivate within yourself will significantly increase, and subsequently, so will the value you bring to others.

Often, the development of any skill and the possibilities we aspire to create are confined by our own limiting thoughts. Be vigilant about the words you speak to yourself.

Ultimately, what matters most is who we choose to be and the impact we have on those around us. At heart, we all want to feel valued and know that we provide value in return.

So, I ask you: Will you choose to be the Value Negotiator?

For more information

- For access to the resources mentioned in the book as well as reader bonuses please visit: thevaluenegotiator.com/playbook

- You can also connect with me here: linkedin.com/in/glinbayley/

- For corporate workshop or speaking enquiries please submit your request to: info@thevaluenegotiator.com

- For salary negotiation guidance please visit: thevalue negotiator.com/SalaryNegotiation